Country Wisdom
&
Folklore Almanac

Edited by

Richard Taylor

Copyright © 2020 Anne Marie Lagram

All rights reserved.

ISBN: 9798649043458

CONTENTS

1 Imbolc – 1st February   Pg 2

2 Vernal Equinox   Pg 11

3 Beltane – 1st May   Pg 19

4 Summer Solstice   Pg 29

5 Lammas – 1st August   Pg 39

6 Autumn Equinox   Pg 51

7 Samhain – 31st October   Pg 59

8 Winter Solstice   Pg 69

9 Curios of the British Isles   Pg 79

Country Wisdom & Folklore Almanac

Celebrating the Cycles of Mother Nature

The Wheel of the Year

Forward

The Country Wisdom & Folklore Almanac is a compilation of folklore, traditions, recipes, country wisdom, stories, eccentricities and superstitions that were first published in the Country Wisdom & Folklore Diary. Year by Year the diary has become more popular but began in a small way meaning that many of you may have missed these first snippets that we shared. The seasonality of the information from these past diaries meant it was perfect to be shared in an Almanac format.

Our Almanac will help you to celebrate and mark the year, through not only the seasons, but also through the Wheel of the Year, which gives us eight points to focus on, with the Solstices and the Equinoxes, the Celtic-rooted celebrations of Beltane (May Day) and Samhain (Halloween) and the Gaelic tradition of Imbolc (early Spring) and Lammas (harvest-time). Though the Wheel of the Year is a relatively new construct each part of it has an older past many of which were celebrated and marked by our ancestors throughout the British Isles according to their own local traditions and customs.

By reading our little Almanac and marking seasonal and significant days throughout the year, you are helping us in our endeavour to keep alive the old ways and celebrate the year.

IMBOLC

1ST FEBRUARY

The wheel has turned once more, returning us to a time of hope and new beginnings. Be thankful for the ever-increasing warmth and light as we leave behind the cold, dark stillness of winter. Make merry, light a candle and feast.

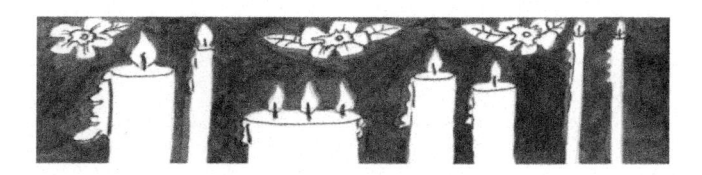

Imbolc

The beginning of February has many different names and customs attributed to it, such as Candlemas, Imbolc and the Feast of the Bride— all of which involve crossover imagery and aspirations. The Celtic word for milk is 'oimelc' from which 'Imbolc' derives. Candles are lit to illuminate winter's darkness and purify the home. Motherhood is celebrated as the first lambs are born and mother's milk flows freely, serving both as nourishment and a bond between mother and baby. It is a good time to meditate on the passing winter and to learn from its harshness so that you are well prepared for the coming year.

This is an excellent time to make your own candles or to decorate those you have bought by carving them or dipping them in melted coloured wax to make them more personal to you. Make soup from root vegetables, potatoes and leafy greens to drink outdoors (in a mug) as you search for those first signs of spring. Dress in white, yellow and green to make you feel brighter and lighter, and scent your home with fragrant oils such as lemon, mandarin, grapefruit and lime to create an uplifting atmosphere for all who dwell there.

A Brigid's Cross is an old Irish symbol which although appearing to be Christian, is more likely to derive from the pagan 'sun wheel'. They are usually made from rushes or straw and comprise of a woven square centre with four radial spokes that are tied at the ends. These crosses act as an amulet against fire and evil and are often hung in houses and barns.

Triple Goddess of the Celts

The Celts had an affinity with the number three – as have many peoples and religions. Three is a number that cannot be subdivided giving it strength and power (unlike the number four which can be split into pairs).

A particularly popular triple goddess of Irish origin, is the three sisters: Brigit the Poetess; Brigit the Smith and Brigit the Doctor – patrons of their respective skills. Amongst the Welsh triads, three queens were associated with King Arthur: Gwenhwyfar, daughter of Cywryd Gwent; Gwenhwyfar, daughter of Gwythyr, and Gwenhwyfar, daughter of Gogfran the Giant. Equally, King Arthur's bloodline had three sisters: Morgan le Fay, Morgause and Elaine, all of whom were considered women of magic and accomplished in many skills.

The idea of a neo triple goddess emerges when Cambridge classicist, Jane Ellen Harrison, inspired by the ancient pagan world, draws on the representation of the 'Fates' and 'Graces' as three divine women. In 1948, in his book, 'The White Goddess', Robert Graves names her aspects as maiden, mother and crone and relates her to the waxing, full and waning moon. This new goddess is celebrated as a nature deity.

Valentine's Day
14th February

Valentine's Day in the village of Waveney in Norfolk, as recounted by Angela Martin from her childhood in the 1960's/70's:

'At dusk there was a knock on the door and the children were sent to open it and on the step was a paper bag full of small gifts and sweets that Jack Valentine had left. Sometimes a string was wrapped around the bag's neck and it would move, we would never see Jack but he was always deemed a bit naughty and very mysterious.'

After reading Angela's recollection we have found out a little bit more about Jack Valentine, who is a particularly well-known figure in Norfolk and Suffolk. Also known as Old Father Valentine or Old Mother Valentine, Jack was a mystery figure who left valentine treats for children and adults alike. The origins of this custom are unclear and most information relates to the early 20th century, although it is said that in Victorian times, in Norfolk Valentine's Eve was as important as Christmas Eve. Snatch was another name given to the mysterious visitor and in this guise he was associated with the mischievous side mentioned by Angela; A knock would be given at the door and the person opening it would see a gift deposited on the doorstep which was then yanked away.

Shrove Tuesday
Between 3rd February & 9th March

Shrove Tuesday always falls forty seven days before Easter Sunday. It is the day prior to the beginning of lent which was traditionally a time of fasting. In Anglo-Saxon times Christians went to confession and were 'shriven' which meant absolved from their sins. The church would ring a bell to call people to confession which came to be known as the 'Pancake Bell'.

The pancake was a good way of using up flour, fat and eggs which were prohibited foods during lent. Pancake recipes have featured in cookery books as far back as 1439 and 'Pasquil's Palin' in 1619, mentions the tradition of tossing panckes:

'And every man and maide doe take their turne, And tosse their Pancakes up for feare they burne.'

There are still many pancake races and shrove-tide games played throughout the country. Westminster School in London holds the annual 'Pancake Greaze'. This is where boys from each 'house' compete to get the biggest piece of a huge pancake that is tossed over a fifteen foot bar by the school chef, in order to win a sovereign. Following the 'Greaze', the Head requests that the Dean grant a holiday for the rest of the day for the boys.

In Scarborough, Yorkshire, street skipping with long ropes takes place on Shrove Tuesday before the annual pancake race.

'If you eat pancakes on 'Goody Tuesday', and grey peas on Ash Wednesday, you will have money in your purse all the year'.

Mothering Sunday
Between 2nd March & 4th April

The fourth Sunday in Lent was a holiday for those working 'in service' and for apprentices. Traditionally it was the day they could go home and visit their mother and was for many the first opportunity they had to go home in their working year. It was customary to take a small gift of a posy of violets or perhaps a simnel cake.

'I'll to thee a simnel bring
Gainst thou go'st a mothering.'

From 'Hesperides'- Herrick 1648.

The Shrewsbury simnel cake was described by Shropshire folklorist Charlotte Burne as 'round and rather flat, with a curiously scalloped upper edge,' and consisted of a rich plum mixture with candied peel, currants, sugar and spices that was encased in a crust made of flour, water and saffron . The fruit mixture was boiled in a cloth for many hours and then the crust was wrapped around it and brushed with egg which was then baked to form a hard crust. Eating a slice of this cake would provide a welcome treat from the Lenten fast.

When servants were allowed to choose when they took a holiday the traditions of this day declined and remained only as a church celebration marking mid-lent and encouraging parishioners to visit their 'mother church.'

Snowdrops

The first snowdrops lift our spirits as we witness these hardy little flowers facing up to the wintery weather reminding us that spring is on its way. Each day, the snowdrop wisely goes to bed early and rises late; by mid-afternoon its flower closes and does not reopen fully again until mid-morning the next day.

> **It is thought unlucky to bring Snowdrops into the house as they brought sickness and death.**

On warm mornings, these delicate flowers provide much needed nectar for bees that have awoken early from their hibernation. They soon get to work pollinating other snowdrops with the pollen dusted on their small bodies. Not far behind the snowdrop, the lesser celandine, with bright shiny little yellow flowers, can be seen on sheltered banks and bordering woodland. A lesser-known plant, whitlow grass whose life cycle from leaf to flower to seed is only a couple of weeks in early March, grows atop mossy walls and sunny sheltered banks. It has small oblong leaves that spread from a central rosette from which a slender stalk rises bearing a cluster of tiny white star-like flowers. Next, wood anemones, also known as wind flowers, crowfoot, thimbleweed and smell fox begin to carpet the ground with swathes of delicate white flowers which sway and nod in the lightest of breeze. The first narcissus make a splendid show of yellow and white, which are the colours associated with very early spring.

The Rain Bird

John Aubrey, a 16th Century English antiquarian, noted that the green woodpecker was used by the druids for divination stating that, 'to this day the country people do divine of raine by their cry.' This bird has many local names, some associated with its supposed power to prophesise rain; Weather Cock, Rain-fowl and Rainpie. Its other names include; Laughing Betsey, Yockel, Yappingale and Yaffle, all of which are derived from its loud, laughing call. Yaffle was such a popular name that it became a verb meaning 'to sound like a woodpecker'. Unlike greater and lesser spotted woodpeckers, the green woodpecker rarely drums on tree trunks, preferring to rely on its vocal skills to attract a mate and make its presence known.

It is a striking bird with bright green plumage and yellow rump and is a ground-feeder with a preference for ants. Its sharp beak and long tongue, which is coated with a sticky secretion, make it easy for it to feast off ant's nests. It favours areas of waste grassland, sheep-grazed pasture and garden lawns where ant colonies thrive.

During March the birds pair up in a monogamous bond that can last for many years. It is believed the pair will roost near to each other over the winter but will not re-establish their relationship until spring.

Brent Knoll, Somerset

Brent Knoll Camp is an Iron Age hill fort situated in the Somerset levels which dominates the flat landscape. It has been inhabited since the Bronze Age and was used as a fortification by Iron Age people as well as the Romans. Several battles have taken place here; one between the Britons and the Anglo-Saxons (possibly involved King Arthur) and another between the Anglo-Saxon Kingdom of Wessex and the Great Heathen Army led by Guthrum the Dane in 875 AD.

According to legend, the hill was created by the Devil when he was carving out Cheddar Gorge and was the result of throwing a handful of rock out towards the sea which landed in the wetlands. It is said to be where Ider, the son of Nuth, who was one of King Arthur's knights, came on a quest to slay three giants who lived there. Before the Somerset Levels were drained, Brent Knoll was an island, known as the Isle (or Mount) of Frogs. The word 'knoll' means a small hill or hilltop. The origin of the name Brent is unclear, but may be derived from the word 'brant', meaning 'steep' in Old English. The view from the top of Brent Knoll is wonderful, with all-round views to the Bristol Channel and Wales on the far shore, Burnham-on-Sea, Brean Down, Weston-Super-Mare, the Mendip Hills and in the distance Glastonbury Tor, the Polden Hills and Bridgwater Bay, with the Quantock Hills and Exmoor beyond.

Since the 1835 Highways Act banned playing football on public highways, many shrove-tide 'mob' football customs ceased but a number of towns such as Alnwick in Northumberland and Ashbourne in Derbyshire have continued the tradition in some form.

VERNAL EQUINOX

21ST or 22ND MARCH

The Spring Equinox, also known as Ostara, is the point when the hours of daylight become greater than those of darkness. Spring is present as we witness spring bulbs, blossom and birds nesting. It is a time when the hare is active and can be seen 'boxing'. In the garden, it is a good time to prepare the ground for seedlings by removing debris and weeds and by turning the sods to aerate the soil.

During Ostara, at this time of balance, aim to achieve equilibrium within your own life. As you tidy- up in your garden, removing autumn and winter debris, do the same within your mind by literally sweeping away the old issues to make room for new things in your life. Sit outside and feel the earth quickening as new life emerges and retain this new spring energy within you.

The Spring Equinox

Also known as the Vernal Equinox and Ostara, this is the first of the four solar festivals of the year. Reference is attributed to Bede, born in the late 7th century, of 'eostre' being a Germanic or Anglo-Saxon word for 'goddess of the dawn'. In the northern hemisphere, the sun rises or dawns in the 'east', a word also derived from 'eostre'. The spring has many references and celebrations featuring mother goddesses of all religions, including Isis, Aphrodite, the Virgin Mary, Cybele and Demeter.

Light and dark are balanced at the point of equinox, but as momentum takes us forward we begin to experience lengthened daylight hours, allowing us truly to leave winter behind. In the fields we see an abundance of new-born lambs suckling from their mothers. It is a time when the land is planted with seed in readiness to bring forth a bountiful crop, birds are mating and the trees grow heavy with blossom and bud.

To celebrate this day, rise early to witness this special sunrise; breakfast on eggs and dairy foods in recognition of new life and motherhood and spoil yourself with a glass of Bucks Fizz. Decorate your table with pots of primroses and scattered blossom. Light a candle to honour the sun, bringing light and warmth. Take time to lose yourself and be still as the springtime flame flickers.

April Fool's Day
1st April

The origins of April Fool's Day are clouded in mystery, although it has been linked with Lud, the Celtic God of Humour. It was also known as All Fools' Day but was colloquially called April Noddy or in parts of Scotland, April Gowk (a name for a cuckoo).

The tradition is thought to have come from Germany in the seventeenth century as no record has been found of this day prior to then. In 1686 John Aubrey referred to the celebration as 'Fooles holy day'. This was the first British reference to All Fools Day. On April 1st 1698, it is recorded that people were tricked into going to the Tower of London to 'see the lions washed'.

Once lasting the whole day it at some point became customary for the 'fooling' to end at midday, but after mid- day the victim should say:

'April Fool's gone past, you're the biggest fool at last!'

During mediaeval times, people would not travel on days that were believed to be 'evil'. In particular, the first Monday in April, which was traditionally thought to be the anniversary of Cain murdering his brother Abel; the second Monday in August, which was associated with the destruction of Sodom and Gomorrah, and the last Monday in December, which was believed to be Judas Iscariot's birthday.
Superstition surrounding these three days continued right up to the nineteenth century.

Easter Customs
Between 22nd March & 25th April

The Christian observance of Lent meant that people had abstained from meat and dairy products for forty days and nights. On Maundy Thursday alms were given to the poor in the form of 'doling' out food such as barley bread. Good Friday required full abstinence from all food except bread. However, a record from East Anglia tells how in 1337 Dame Katherine de Norwich, the widow of an exchequer official, fed thirteen poor in her household each day throughout Lent and on Good Friday gave them 'wastel' which was one of the finest breads.

One of many Easter Monday traditions is a 'bottle-kicking scramble', in Hallaton, Leicestershire. The custom is said to have begun when two ladies were saved from a stampeding bull by a hare which distracted it. In gratitude to God, they donated money to the church on the understanding that every Easter Monday, the vicar would provide a hare pie, twelve penny loaves, and two barrels of beer for the poor of the village. However this generosity led to the villagers fighting for the food and drink and so the tradition of an annual 'scramble' had begun. When in 1790 the rector tried to ban the custom because he thought it too pagan he found the words 'no pie, no parson' scrawled on the wall of the vicarage, making him relent.

The Sun was said to 'jump or dance for joy' on Easter morning resulting in many people seeking out special vantage points to witness the Sun's celebration.

The Biddenden Maids

The Biddenden Maids were conjoined twins, supposedly born in 1100 in Biddenden, Kent. They are said to have lived for 34 years and on their death they bequeathed five plots of land to the village, known as the Bread and Cheese Lands. The income from this land was then used to dole out food and drink to the poor of the village during Easter. Since at least 1775 the dole has included Biddenden Cakes, a hard biscuit with an image of the two twins imprinted on them. Although the food distribution is known to have taken place from at least 1605, there is no record of the sisters prior to 1770 and many believe the story to be mere folklore. Edward Hasted, a historian from the 18th century thought the story 'a vulgar tradition'.

Throughout the 19th century despite the doubts the legend of the sisters grew and 'throngs of rowdy people' descended on the village every Easter. In the late Victorian era, further investigations were carried out which led to the belief that although the story of the conjoined twins could well be true it was more probable they were from 16th rather than the 12th century.

In 1907 the Bread and Cheese Lands were sold for housing which further enriched the cake fund, providing the widows and pensioners of Biddenden with cheese, bread and tea at Easter and with cash payments at Christmas. Biddenden cakes continue to be given to the poor of Biddenden each Easter, and are sold as souvenirs to visitors.

Easter Monday & Easter Tuesday

One popular rural custom which took place at this time was 'heaving'. On 'Heaving Monday', women would 'heave' aloft a chair decorated with ribbons and flowers three times and spin it around, while on 'Heaving Tuesday', women would be heaved aloft by the men. Afterwards, both heaving parties would be rewarded with money for the men and a kiss for the women. The woman chosen to sit in the chair would be given a posy of flowers dipped in water and sprinkled over her feet as a blessing. If you did not want to be hoisted skywards by the merry troop of 'heavers', it was customary to give a gift of food or money. It was often the case that servants would try to 'heave' those they were in service to, in the hope of gaining financial reward.

Afterwards, following evening prayer, parishioners would often join together and feast on bread, cheese and ale provided by the church or local landowner. This was generally known as the 'church-feast' although in Berrington in Shropshire it was called a 'love-feast'.

St George's Day, 23rd April

The legend of St George and the Dragon in England is believed to date back to the twelfth century, when crusaders returned from battle having invoked his help as they fought. It is uncertain how the story of St George slaying a Dragon to save a princess came about but it became known as a tale of a Christian soldier fighting against evil for his faith. Historically it appears that he may have been a high-ranking officer who was martyred in Palestine in AD 303. It is thought that Edward III made him England's patron saint in 1350 when he founded the Order of the Garter in St George's name. The cult of St George in England advanced in the reign of Henry V, who was a devout soldier king. Over the years St George's day has been kept by wearing a red rose, by mummers including him as the patriotic knight in their plays and by flying the English flag, which is known as St George's cross, and was the banner he carried into battle. However times have changed and the day is often overlooked by many people.

John Aubrey, doubted the authenticity of the story of St George and wrote in the 1680's:

'To save a mayd, St George the Dragon slew,
A pretty tale if all is told true,
Most say there are no dragons; and this say'd
There was no George; Pray God there was a mayd.'

Melangell & the Hare

Melangell (pronounced mell-an-geth) ran away from home because she was to be married against her will. She settled in a beautiful and isolated valley at the head of the Afon Tanat, in Montgomeryshire. One day the Prince of Powys, Brochwel Ysgythrog, was out hunting hares with his hounds. A hare ran under Melangell's skirts to hide and the hounds drew back. The Prince was immediately affected by her presence and beauty. He asked to marry her, but on her refusal, he granted the land to Melangell as a sanctuary and bade her to build a convent there.

The Prince swore not to hunt hare and to this day it is considered that ill- omen will befall anyone who hunts hares in Melangell's valley. She is the patroness and protector of hares, whom she called 'her lambs'.

It is believed that if you see a hare being pursued, call 'Melangell be with thee' and the hare will escape. She was made into a saint and in the Welsh calendar she is commemorated on 31st January and 4th May. A beautiful tiny chapel at Pennant Melangell, stands as a place of pilgrimage with images, carvings and artwork depicting Melangell and her beloved hare set amongst a ring of ancient yews and in a breathtaking tranquil landscape.

BELTANE

1ST MAY

Beltane marked the beginning of summer in rural communities. Fires would be lit in the fields and animals driven between them to purify and protect them before they were moved to their summer home in the upland pastures. The first of May has been marked as a special day for a long time and, in many communities, is being revived as a celebratory day. The Fire Festival in Edinburgh is a spectacular event which takes place on 1st May.

The fires were seen as a way of reinforcing the sun as it reached its midsummer peak. In Nottinghamshire and Derbyshire, the midsummer fires were called 'belfires'. Herbs and small oak branches were often thrown into the fire and, as the fires died down, it was considered good luck to jump through the flames.

Beltane

Call out 'Hey Nonny Nonny' to all—and to the beautiful oaks in our world! Welcome the Green Man as he passes, bringing the promise of summer.

Now the bright morning-star, Day's harbinger,
Comes dancing from the East, and leads with her
The flowery May, who from her green lap throws
The yellow cowslip and the pale primrose.
Hail, bounteous May, that dost inspire
Mirth, and youth, and warm desire!
Woods and groves are of thy dressing;
Hill and dale doth boast thy blessing.
Thus we salute thee with our early song,
And welcome thee, and wish thee long.

John Milton, 'Song on a May Morning'

Mayday customs include walking the circuit of one's property, known as 'beating the bounds', and repairing fences and boundary markers. Light a bel (goodly) fire and celebrate this most ancient of festivals. Be outdoors eating, drinking and making merry.

> **In the early 19th century, the Halliwell (Holy Well) Wake was held on 1st May in the hamlet of Rorrington on the Shropshire/Wales border. The local people met at the holy well on the hillside at Rorrington Green and decorated the well with green boughs, flowers and rushes. A maypole was erected while a fife, drum and fiddle played; the people danced and frolicked around the hill, followed by feasting, drinking and more dancing.**

'Obby 'oss Day

'Obby 'oss Day is an ancient tradition and spring rite that takes place on 1st May in the lovely little coastal village of Padstow, Cornwall.

Two 'osses, one blue and one red, are released from their 'pub' stables (each pub having an allegiance to a particular 'oss). The blue 'oss (the colour of the original 'oss) is released an hour before the red 'oss (the peace 'oss). The 'osses dance, prance and twirl through the narrow streets and around the harbour; visiting the church and maypole along the way, accompanied by music and a unique song, much to the delight of the spectators. Each 'oss costume consists of a snapping head with an oval body and skirt. A 'teaser' dances in front of the 'osses, who respond by lifting up their skirts. The significance of this act is not known, although it is thought to be connected with fertility and May Day rituals. It was believed that the 'oss would try to capture a maiden under its skirt and that she would become pregnant that same year. People who were born in Padstow dress in white, and wear either a red or blue sash or ribbons, depending on the loyalties of their family.

All of this is part of the folklore and fun associated with the day and perhaps gives an insight into some of the many celebrations that would have taken place for Beltane across the country. A visit to Padstow to join in the celebrations is strongly recommended.

The Green Man

The Green Man is also known as Jack-in-the-Green, the May King and the Wildman of the Woods. His guise is usually foliate whether it is of a face disgorging leaves in a church carving, or a full figure hidden by leaves dancing in a May Day procession

He is the guardian of the trees, bringer of spring and recently a symbol of the new 'green movement'. It is believed that he may be present as Robin Hood, Herne the Hunter, Merlin, the Green Knight and even John Barleycorn amongst others, all of whom carry the spirit of the woods.

He survives all year from spring's pale green buds to the dark green evergreens of the winter. Although it is unclear when, why and even where this image comes from, it is undoubtedly ancient and was given new interest in Victorian times when images and carvings were used to decorate and adorn buildings. It is believed that a Green Man hung over an outside doorway provides protection to those within.

Places to see the Green Man include; The Green Man Festival in Clun, Shropshire and the Jack in the Green Festival in Hastings, Sussex, both held on May bank holiday Monday. He can also be seen at many other May Day festivals taking place throughout the country in a variety of guises.

Oak Apple Day
29th May

Oak Apple Day, also known as Restoration day, is celebrated on the 29th May to commemorate the restoration of King Charles ll to the throne in 1660. It became customary for people to wear a sprig of oak to show their loyalty to the king and woe betide anyone who didn't wear one as it showed them to be anti-royalist. Punishment for this was usually meted out by local people who whipped people with nettles, pelted them with very rotten eggs, bumped them or even gave them a pinch and so the day also became known as Nettling Day, Bumping Day and Pinching or Pinch Bum Day depending where you lived in the country.

Much of the 'fun' was in schools and children would sing rhymes whilst begging from door to door such as;

'Shig-shag, penny a rag, bring his head in Cromwell's bag. All up in a bundle'

And so the day was also often known as Shig-Shag or Shick-Shack Day.

The connection of the oak to the king relates to the time he hid in an oak tree at Boscobel in Staffordshire when he was being chased by Cromwell's puritan army following his defeat at the battle of Worcester in 1651. Many pubs became named the Royal Oak after the restoration and their sign showed the king amongst the foliage of an oak tree. Although not widely observed now, the day is still celebrated in Castleton, Derbyshire, Great Wishford , Wiltshire, Aston - on- Clun, Shropshire, St Neots, Cornwall and at the Royal Chelsea Hospital as Charles ll was their founder.

Whitsunday

A popular day for baptisms, Whitsunday falls on the seventh Sunday after Easter, making it a moveable feast. It was a welcome holiday with many outdoor events taking place including walks, wakes, Morris dancing and fêtes. In Cambridgeshire, it was known as the day for eating the first gooseberry pie and the first of the new potatoes. Goosnargh cakes from Lancashire, resembling shortbread but flavoured with caraway and coriander, with a thick sugary crust, were consumed in great numbers—with a recorded 50,000 being sold at one shilling per dozen. It was a time for new clothes for many, or making old outfits new ready for the coming summer. People, particularly children, wearing their best clothes would take part in Whit walks and processions organised by the church.

Celebrations continued throughout the week as most people had a few days' or even a week's holiday. These dats soon became adopted as a factory shut-down week for many workers. In Cambridge, 'Mother Shipton's Holiday' was held on Whit Wednesday. It is recorded that those working in laundries would be given rum in their tea as she was considered a 'patron saint' of the laundress. Brass band competitions were commonly held on Whit Friday.

The Whitsun song was sung as part of the merriment of this holiday.

Now be the merry Whitsun come
Sing O, sing hillo;
Bring out tabor, bring out drum,
Heigh ho, heigh ho!
Arbours for maidens,
Alleys for the men,
While the bells are ringing,
Whitsun's come again.
Sing, sing heigh ho!

The Cuckoo (*Cuculus canorus*)

This traditional English folk song gives an alternative view of this much- maligned bird.

The Cuckoo is a pretty bird, she sings as she flies.
She bringeth good tidings, she telleth no lies
She sucketh white flowers for to keep her voice clear
And she never sings 'cuckoo' till summer draweth near.

There are many sayings about its call: if you are young, the number of times you hear its call tells you the time you will marry; if you are married, then it indicates the arrival of your next child; if you are old, it indicates how much longer you have to live; and your state of health when you hear the cuckoo is how it will remain for the year.

It is believed that, because the cuckoo is so busy predicting things, it does not have time to build its own nest to lay eggs and to bring up chicks. In Wales, it is considered unlucky to hear its call before April 6th and in England it is considered unlucky to hear the cuckoo after Midsummer's Day. On hearing its call you should take a coin from your pocket and spit on it for good fortune. Sadly, this once familiar migrant visitor is in decline. Before people learned about migration, it was believed that the cuckoo became a hawk and hibernated in hillsides.

Hawthorn (*Crataegus monogyna*)

During the land enclosures between the 16th and 18th centuries, nearly 200,000 miles of hawthorn hedges were planted. This fast growing, sturdy and spiny species provides an almost impenetrable barrier when it is cut and laid. Hawthorn blossom features in many May Day celebrations, however according to superstition, hawthorn blossom must never be brought into the home and to do so would be to court disaster. One plausible reason why is that its chemical 'smell' is the same as when living tissue first begins to decay; perhaps the smell echoes the time when bodies were laid out in the home before burial and the people were much more familiar with the smell of death.

Hawthorn trees are supposed to be a favourite of witches who are said to be able to transform themselves into one at will. Hawthorn is sacred to the fey folk and if you see oak, ash and hawthorn growing together, it is said that you may be granted permission to see them. Beware of sitting beneath a hawthorn tree during the month of May as it may mean that you will be lost to the unknown, mysterious fey world forever.

Ramsons (Allium ursinum)

Ramsons, or Wild Garlic, are extremely evasive and can be found widely carpeting the floor of deciduous woodlands. They have an extremely pungent aroma and it is thought the name ramsons is derived from an older word 'ram' meaning 'rank'. The leaves and flowers are both edible and can be used for flavouring soups or even eaten raw as salad leaves. A bulbous plant with white flowers and broad flat leaves, ramsons flower April to June.

One nice recipe to try is Potato and Ramsons Soup

Twenty young fresh ramsons leaves
Two large potatoes
Butter
Vegetable stock powder
Salt & pepper
Handful of peas
Splash of milk

Dice the potatoes and place into a saucepan. Cover the potatoes with water and add a knob of butter and half a teaspoon of vegetable stock powder. Bring to the boil and simmer gently for about twenty minutes. Wash the ramsons thoroughly and slice thinly. When the potatoes are cooked add the ramsons leaves together with a splash of milk. Leave to cool slightly and then liquidize in the saucepan using a hand-held blender. Add a handful of peas and season to taste with salt and freshly ground black pepper. Thin the soup down with some extra water or milk if necessary. Serve hot.

Madron Well, Cornwall

Madron Well would originally have been a source of fresh water and the 'genus loci' or spirit who dwelt there venerated. The earliest reference to this site was in 1640, when the 'cripple John Trelill' came and bathed once a week for three weeks in May, he slept on a nearby mound called St. Maddern's Bed and was cured. The area has a history of spiritual use by both Christian's and Pagans. Up until recently, the local Methodists would hold an open-air service on the first Sunday in May whilst local Pagans congregate there to honour Mother Earth.

A tree growing near the well became known as 'The Cloughtie Tree'. It was a traditional custom at healing wells to tie 'clouties' or pieces of rag, torn from a part of the body where the injury or hurt was, and tie them on a tree close to the well and as the material disintegrated, so the hurt would go away.

The bapistry was, and is still used today to plunge babies in; three times through the water widdershins (anti-clockwise) to keep good health. The chapel is dedicated to St. Maddern, who is the patron saint of Madron Church.

Beyond the ruined chapel is a tree lined avenue or processional route, which on a breezy day encourages the trees to communicate with you by clacking their branches and twigs together

> **In 1871, Robert Hunt recorded that maidens would visit Madron Well on each of the first three Thursdays in May. They would make a cross to float on the water. The number of bubbles rising up would indicate the number of years before matrimony.**

Country Wisdom & Folklore Almanac

SUMMER SOLSTICE
20th – 22nd June

The Summer Solstice is also known as Litha and refers to the Anglo-Saxon word for the months of June and July. During the next few days, the wheel of the year turns back in favour of shortened days and lengthened nights. Even though we begin to move closer to winter, the best of summer is yet to come. Weather permitting, it is a beautiful day to watch the sun rise and experience the early morning stillness during the mild chill of daybreak.

Midsummers Eve
19th – 21st June

On Midsummer's Eve people lit bonfires on hills, in villages, on commons and on farm land. In some places this was known as 'setting the watch.' Many purposes have been attributed to these midsummer fires: to keep evil spirits at bay, bring fertility, purify, give power to the sun and mark the change in the year. Often fire was taken from one bonfire to another by lighting torches. There was a tradition of jumping the bonfire which was said to bring good luck. It was also thought that the highest jump indicated the height the crops would grow to during the year.

This time of the year also became known as Johnsmas because the church celebrated St John's day, probably as a way of allowing traditional ways to co-exist with Christianity.

In the late 14th-century, John Mirk of Lilleshall Abbey, Shropshire, gives the following description: 'At first, men and women came to church with candles and other lights and prayed all night long. In the process of time, however, men left such devotion and used songs and dances and fell into lechery and gluttony turning the good, holy devotion into sin.'

In an attempt to stop such lewd practices the church ordained that people should fast on the evening before midsummer. In some places sun wheels were made. These were wheels covered in hemp, smeared with pitch and then set alight and rolled down hills.

The Summer Solstice
20th – 22nd June

Golowan (also Goluan or Gol-Jowan) is the Cornish language word for the Midsummer celebrations in Cornwall. These celebrations involved lighting bonfires (known as 'Tansys Golowan' in Cornish) and performing associated rituals. This festival was described by Dr William Borlase in 1754, in his book, 'Antiquities of Cornwall': 'In Cornwall, the festival Fires, called Bonfires, are kindled on the Eve of St. John the Baptist and St. Peter's Day; and Midsummer is thence, in the Cornish tongue, called 'Goluan', which signifies both light and rejoicing. At these Fires the Cornish attend with lighted torches, tarr'd and pitch'd at the end, and make their perambulations round their Fires, and go from village to village carrying their torches before them; and this is certainly the remains of the Druid superstition, for 'faces praeferre', to carry lighted torches, was reckoned a kind of Gentilism, and as such particularly prohibited by the Gallick Councils: they were in the eye of the law 'accensores facularum', and thought to sacrifice to the devil, and to deserve capital punishment.'

The midsummer bonfire ceremonies were revived at St Ives in 1929 by The Old Cornwall Society and spread to other societies across Cornwall as far as Kit Hill near Callington. Since 1991, The Golowan Festival in Penzance has revived many ancient customs and has become a major arts and culture festival, with a central event known as 'Mazey Day', in late June.

Midsummer Faeries

Midsummer was considered a particularly active time for the fey realm and people feared coming across faerie activity and being cursed by them. Children were particularly considered at risk of being taken by the faeries.

'Come away, O human child! To the waters and the wild, with a faery hand in hand, for the world's more full of weeping than you can understand.'

In Ireland, faeries are often known as the 'little people', the 'gentry', or the 'neighbours' as a sign of endearment and respect. People actively go out of their way to avoid faerie paths and digging into faerie mounds and recently a planned road was rerouted because it would have interfered in a known faerie site. There are also examples of people removing corners off their home for fear of blocking the faerie path and building a back door that directly aligns with the front door, both of which can then be left open at night to let the faeries pass through.

People built 'Baal' fires at midsummer, to celebrate the strengthening sun and also to frighten spirits away. However, the faeries were able to put out fires by passing round them so fast that they created a whirlwind and the only way to stop them was if the fire spat at them.

At the Rollright Stones in Oxfordshire it was traditional to gather around the King Stone and 'bleed the elder' (meaning to cut it) on Midsummer Eve. The King Stone would then reportedly move 'his head'. This is because a Danish king and his men, who on fighting for the English crown, asked an elder tree witch what their fate would be. The elder witch replied by turning the king and his men into stones, preventing them from going into battle. The stone circle is surrounded by elder trees to this day.

Fairlop Fair
First Friday in July

According to ancient custom;

'Gay Fairlop' was held on 'the first Friday in July on the borders of Hainault or Epping Forrest, and drew together an immense number of persons. The block-makers, sail-makers, mast-makers, as usual, preceded to the forest at an early hour in their amphibious-looking 'frigates', mounted on carriages, rigged out like ships and decorated with colours. Each of these vehicles was drawn by six horses, gaily dressed out, and the wives of the men in their holiday gear followed in open landaus. The booths and shows were not so numerous as on former occasions, and the restriction of the fair to one day by the Essex magistrates has sadly diminished the profits of those who cater for the public. The Gipsies were uncommonly numerous; but the thimble and pea-riggers were dispersed by the police, and quitted the fair amidst the hootings of the people...the conduct of the assembled thousands was marked by the greatest good humour and decorum, and there was not a single police charge arising out of 'the first Friday in July.'

Illustrated London News 15th July 1843

The fair was held around an oak tree that was reputed to be thirty six feet in circumference, and was a focal point over many years but it was sadly damaged by a fire, believed to have been started by picnickers in 1805. The oak was blown down in 1820 and its wood was used to make the pulpit of St. Pancras Church, Euston Road, London.

> **'In 1315, on the day after the anniversary of the moving of St. Swithin's body (into the church) namely the 15th July, such was the deluge of rain, that rivers overflowed their banks to an awesome degree, submerging crops and rushing through houses, drowning men, women and children. No survivor could recall such a flood, nor such a famine that followed.'**
> **Robert de Graystane, c.1336.**

Common Riding, Langholm
Last Friday of July

Common riding is an annual event celebrated in Langholm, as well as in many of the other Scottish border towns. It dates back to the time when it was necessary to clearly define communal or 'common' areas of land using beacons, cairns and pits to ensure that the townsfolk would retain certain rights, such as digging for peat.

In olden times the boundaries were never actually formally 'ridden', but horses and riding now form the major part of the celebrations. 'Ride-outs' take place the preceding day up and around the hills and through the town. On the day itself, the Cornet (Master of Ceremonies) and his riders gallop up the Kirk Wynd and to the Monument. 'Langholm's Great Day' always takes place on the last Friday in July and begins with a parade of the flute band and ends when the Cornet hands back the flag in front of the town hall.

One of the features of the Langholm Common Riding is the quaint and unique set of emblems that are carried aloft throughout the street procession: the barley banna and sa't herring (a salted herring which is pinned to a bannock); a spade (for cutting sods and clearing pits); a Scotch thistle and a floral crown.

The Faery Coffins Mystery

In 1836 seventeen tiny coffins were found by three boys out 'rabbiting' at Arthur's Seat in Edinburgh. They became known as 'fairy coffins' and to this day no one is sure why they were there or who made them.

This is part of the account from the London Times, July 20, 1836:
'In the coffins were miniature wooden figures. They were dressed differently in both style and material. There were two tiers of eight coffins each, and a third one begun, with one coffin. The extraordinary datum, which has especially made mystery here: That the coffins had been deposited singly, in the little cave, and at intervals of many years. In the first tier, the coffins were quite decayed, and the wrappings had moldered away. In the second tier, the effects of age had not advanced so far. And the top coffin was quite recent looking.'

Fewer than half of the coffins survived because the boys 'pelted them at each other' in fun not realising their potential importance. Those that survived became part of a collection kept by Robert Frazier, a jeweller, who put them on display in his private museum. On his death they were auctioned as 'the celebrated Lilliputian coffins found on Arthur's Seat, 1836,' and sold for just over £4. In 1901 a set of eight, together with their contents, were donated to the National Museum of Scotland by their then-owner, Christina Couper of Dumfriesshire.

Speculation regarding the coffins was that they were 'mimic' burials, as sometimes took place when Scottish sailors were lost at sea and no body was recovered, and that perhaps a similar motive was at hand, or as a means of giving rest to the souls of the seventeen victims of the grave robbers and murders Burke and Hare, who were active at the time the coffins have been dated to.

Meadowsweet (Filipendula ulmaria)

Meadowsweet likes boggy damp conditions and can often be found growing along the banks of streams and rivers. It is a tall plant that can reach 2-3 feet in height and it flowers during the summer months. The sweetness attributed to it arises from dense clusters of tiny white flowers which release a heady scent.

It is believed the floors of the apartments belonging to Queen Elizabeth I were strewn with meadowsweet to make them fragrant. It was used medicinally as a cure for stomach complaints by preparing an infusion of one ounce of the herb to three quarters of a pint of boiling water. The dose is about a teacupful as needed. It is rich in magnesium and iron.

Meadowsweet

Meadowsweet can also be used for making beer. Equal quantities of meadowsweet, dandelion and agrimony should be boiled together for twenty minutes in double the quantity of water. Add two pounds of sugar to each gallon of the strained liquid, together with an ounce of yeast and the juice of a lemon. Leave to ferment and bottle later.

Well Dressing

In ancient times, wells were venerated because they brought life to the villages in the form of clean spring water. Spirits, usually the local deities, were associated with the wells. These guardians were honoured by the people who left offerings and garlands of greenery at the well-head.
As Christianity spread, the worship of 'fountains' was deplored, however the church had to compromise its own thinking to suit the people and began to associate saints with local wells and the custom of 'well dressing' in veneration of the saints was established.

'Well dressing' is still very popular in Derbyshire, when throughout the summer months many villages create beautiful pictures and patterns made of flowers around their wells. These brief, living tributes have become a type of folk art which attracts many visitors who admire the skill involved and enjoy the occasion.

Tissington is one of the Derbyshire villages that is particularly famous and can trace the custom back to 1349, when the village was the only one to escape the scourge of the 'black death'. This miracle was attributed to their pure water supply.

Ashbourne, Buxton, Eyam and Tideswell are amongst the many Derbyshire villages to continue this tradition. Bisley in Gloucestershire and Endon in Staffordshire also follow the custom.

Morris Dancing

This form of dancing can be traced back to the Middle Ages. Traditionally, these ritual dances can only be performed by men, although there is evidence to suggest that women may have joined in.

The dancers are known as 'teams' or 'sides' and some of the oldest and most established ones are based in Abingdon, Bampton, Headington Quarry and Chipping Camden, all of which are in the Cotswold area.

Morris men wear particular attire known to their team, often white shirts, white fitted breaches and bells attached to their legs. Many incorporate colourful ribbons and flowers into their headwear. In their hands they may carry handkerchiefs or sticks which are used as part of the dance.

Each team usually comprises of six members, a fool and sometimes a hobby horse. They dance to music provided by their own musicians, often with a fiddle, accordion and a drum.

Many believe that the origins of Morris Dancing date back to pagan times and may have been used to celebrate ancient rites. Some Morris sides blacken their faces, possibly indicating a 'Moorish' origin. It is thought that the name 'Morris' may even be a corruption of the word 'Moorish'. Others believe the blackened face was just a way to disguise the dancer so that out of work labourers in the 17th and 18th centuries could anonymously supplement their income during lean times.

Abbots Bromley Horn Dance
The first Monday after September 4th

Abbots Bromley Horn Dance is certainly one of the oldest surviving ceremonies in Britain, and is possibly the oldest. It takes place in the Staffordshire village of Abbots Bromley each year on Wakes Monday at the beginning of September, although earliest records of the dance say it used to take place on Twelfth Day, after Christmas.

Robert Plot, in his book 'Natural History of Staffordshire' (1686), wrote:

> *'a sort of sport, which they celebrated at Christmas (on New Year and Twelft-day) called the Hobby-horse dance, from a person that carryed the image of a horse between his leggs ..... and in his hand a bow and arrow ..... which made a snapping noise as he drew it to and fro, keeping time with the Musick; with this Man danced 6 others, carrying on their shoulders as many Rain deers heads, 3 of them painted white, and 3 red ..... with which they danced the Hays and other Country dances. To this Hobby-horse dance there also belong'd a pot which was kept by turnes, by 4 or 5 of the cheif of the Town ..... who provided Cakes and Ale to put in this pot; all people who had any kindness for the good intent of the Institution of the sport, giving pence a piece for themselves and families; and so forraigners too, that came to see it: with which Mony ..... they not only repaired their Church but kept their poore too.'*

The Antlers, still used today, have been carbon dated to the eleventh century.

Harvest

In the past, the harvest was not a mechanised affair as it is now, but a labourous toil for men, women and children. It was often considered extremely unlucky to cut the last sheaf of the corn, since it was believed that the spirits of the crop would be hiding there, taking refuge from the scythes. Often avenues of corn would be left to allow the spirits safe passage from one field to another.

There were several ways of dealing with the last remaining stalks to ensure that no one person could be identified as taking the final cut. In some regions several men would hold up the remaining corn as a 'neck' and would shout, 'I haven't, I haven't, I haven't', and this was known as 'crying the neck'.

In Wiltshire, as the last sheaf was cut it would be held aloft on a pitchfork and the labourers would all shout,:

Well ploughed, well sowed, well harrowed, well mowed and all safely carted to the barn with nary a load throwed! Hip-hip-hip-hooray!'

The 22p stamp of the special 'Folklore' Royal Mail issue of 1981 appears to show a man holding a 'neck' in a Lammas celebration.

The horses and the wagon pulling the very last load would be adorned with garlands and colourful ribbons. The end of all the hard work would be celebrated with much gaiety, singing and dancing. A special super would be eaten and thanks given to a successful harvest.

John Barleycorn

John Barleycorn was the personification of the harvest and is remembered in this ancient song where we hear of the sacrifice made by him, so that we may have our harvest. It was first recorded in 1568 by a Scottish merchant by the name of George Bannatyne. Recorded below is a later version.

There were three men come out of the west, their fortunes for to try,
And these three men made a solemn vow, John Barleycorn must die. They
ploughed, they sown, they harrowed him in,
And lay earth upon his head.
But these three men made a solemn vow, John Barleycorn was dead.

They let him lie for a very long time till the rains from heaven did fall.
And little Sir John sprang up his head and so amazed them all.
They let him stand till midsummer's day and he looks both pale & wan.
Then little Sir John's grown a long, long beard and so become a man.

They hired men with the sharp-edged scythes to cut him off at the knee,
They rolled him and tied him around the waist,
Treated him most barbarously,
They hired men with the sharp-edged forks to prick him to the heart. And
the loader has served him worse than that,
For he's bound him to the cart.

They wheeled him around & around the field till they came into the barn,
And there they make a their solemn vow of poor John Barleycorn.
They hired men with the crab tree sticks to cut him skin from bone.
And the miller has served him worse than that,
For he's ground him between two stones.

Here's to little Sir John in a nut-brown bowl and brandy in the glass.
Little Sir John in the nut-brown bowl, proved the stronger man at last.
And the huntsman he can't hunt the fox nor loudly blow his horn.
And the tinker he can't mend his kettles and pots,
Without a bit of Barleycorn.

Barnacle Geese *(Branta Leucopsis)*

Barnacle Geese are members of the Branta family of mainly black geese. They breed in the Arctic islands of the North Atlantic, and many thousands spend the winter on the west coasts of Scotland and Ireland.

Geraldus Cambrensis, writing in The History and Topography of Ireland (1187), noted:

'I have seen many times and with my own eyes more than a thousand of these small bird-like creatures, hanging from a single log upon the sea shore'.

The geese were once thought to come from barnacles, rather than eggs, possibly because they were never seen in summer, but 'mysteriously' appeared fully grown in winter, especially in coastal margins. This led to the church allowing eaten during Lent, when other meat was not allowed, as they were designated as fish!

Geraldus writes:

'Accordingly in some parts of Ireland bishops and religious men eat them without sin during a fasting time, regarding them as not being flesh, since they were not born of flesh'.

It was not until 1215 that the Pope ruled the Barnacle Goose was, in fact, a bird and not a fish.

On the Solway Firth the geese were known as Rood Geese, as their arrival coincided with the Rood Fayre, held on 14th September.

Droveways

A droveway is a road that was used to herd livestock long distances from one place to another, usually to market. These routes are often ancient, some dating from the Bronze Age and many dating back to well before mediaeval times. The roads were characteristically wide to accommodate herds and were often deeply set, with high hedgerows either side, to assist in channelling the herds safely. Often they became known as 'the long acre'.

The term 'drover' was used to describe people who travelled long distances with herds; whereas 'driver' described people who moved herds locally from one pasture to another. The place where a drover spent the night was called 'the castle'. Often, country place names that include the word 'castle' refer to these drovers' resting places rather than places where castles were located.

Narrow strips of land called 'slingets' were used as overnight holding pens. Dogs were often used to help move the herds and there are several accounts of them being able to retrace the exact path home by themselves once the destination had been reached. The drover had to have a great deal of skill, bravery and control to ensure large herds were looked after so they were safe, fed and watered on journeys that could last weeks or even months and to keep them in good condition for selling on. The last recorded 'drove' of cattle was in Wales in 1870.

Hop Picking

Hops were introduced to England during the early fifteenth century by the Dutch and as a result had the effect of turning traditional ales into beer. After some initial resistance, this new bitter drink became very popular and hop production increased to meet demand, so much so that hops became a major part of the agriculture of fourteen counties. Kent was particularly known for hop production and is said to be where the first plants were grown.

The picking season relied heavily on migrant workers and whole families from London would 'go a hopping' to Kent in time for the season, which began in late August or early September. Left to their own device, hop bines will spread and attach themselves to anything they can cling to, but when cultivated they are trained to grow up poles and along wires, which makes their harvest more accessible. Generations of hop pickers from particular families would often visit the same farm each year. According to one labourer: 'The smell of hops was overpowering and a few people, my mother included, felt sick and faint for the first few days until we became immune to the smell'.

At the end of the season, there was a hop picker's feast—those new to picking would be bundled head first into hop bins, known as 'cribbing', and a hop king and queen would be crowned.

Corn Dolly

Twisting and plaiting straw to make effigies and other objects has been practised all over the world and is closely linked to harvest thanksgiving. In the British Isles, the men who brought in the harvest traditionally made a human-like form out of the last wheat standing. This tradition developed to become a decorative pastoral craft often practised by women. Crafting these symbols of good luck and fertility, which reflected superstitious beliefs, also enabled them to earn a small extra income. In its purest form, the corn dolly was used to thank Mother Earth for the harvest.

'Tis but a thing of straw' they say,
Yet even straw can sturdy be
Plaited into a doll like me.
And in the days of long ago
To help the seeds once more to grow
I was an offering to the gods.
A very simple way indeed
Of asking them to intercede
That barn and granary o'erflow
At harvest time, with fruit and corn
To fill again Amalthea's horn.'

Harvest in Dorset

The writer & poet William Barnes of Dorset (died 1886) is an excellent source relating to old harvest customs.

'In the day appointed for the celebration of the harvest, the labourers from the several farms attended afternoon service in the parish church, dressed in their best clothes, the church being decorated in the usually seasonable manner. The entrance-gates of the principal farms were likewise decorated with an arch of evergreen, flowers, corn, etc., crowned with a sickle and scythe swathed in bands of wheat barley, the whole surmounted by appropriate mottoes'. 'When the wheat is all ripe the harvest begin, the farmer the fruits of the earth gather in; in the mornings as soon as the reap hooks are grind, we repair to the field for to reap and to bind'. 'When the harvest is over to our master's we will steer, and wet a good supper with a drink of strong beer'.

An extract from an account about the last day of harvest;

'When the last load was ricked the labourers, male and female, the swarthy reaper and the sun-burnt hay-maker, the saucy boy who had not seen twelve summers and the stiff horny-handed old mower who had borne the toil of fifty, all made a happy groupe, and went with singing and loud-laughing to the harvest-home supper at the farmhouse, where they were expected by the good mistress, dressed in a quilted petticoat and a linsey-wolsey apron, with shoes fastened by large silver buckles which extended over her foot like a pack-saddle on a donkey'.

AUTUMNAL EQUINOX
BETWEEN 21ST & 24TH SEPTEMBER

The Autumn Equinox marks the beginning of autumn and it is often known as the second harvest. Foremost in our ancestor's minds was to preserve as much food as they could to make it last throughout the coming months. Preserves and pickles were the best way to keep vegetables and fruits in a state fit for consumption and were looked forward to because they 'pepped-up' bland foods and disguised the taste of foods that had gone past their best. Pickles were particularly valued by sailors as they provided vitamin c and helped prevent scurvy.

The Corn Supper

The Autumn Equinox was seen as the time of the second harvest, the final gathering of the year, when every last useful scrap was gathered in and stored to sustain the community through the barren months ahead; it was also a time to celebrate the end of a job well done. In Northumberland, a 'kern baby', constructed from corn and bedecked with flowers in the shape of a person, would lead the procession of reapers making their way to the harvest celebrations. Sometimes, the 'kern baby' would be taken into the fields and attached to a pole for the last day of reaping. In other communities the 'kern baby' would take the form of an actual person, called the 'maiden', or the 'ivy girl'. A young woman would be dressed with ribbons and carried in triumph to the sound of Northumberland pipes, fiddles and drums. The feasting that followed traditionally sat master and servant together, to celebrate the 'harvest home'.

Following the Protestant Reformation in the sixteenth century, these colourful harvest celebrations were superseded by more sombre recompense. The hard work of the labourers would be rewarded with a loaf and a payment of six pennies. Eventually the church began to accept the need of communities for merriment and began the tradition of hosting a corn or harvest supper.

Michaelmas Day
29th September

A lovely old recipe for this day is Michaelmas Dumplings to use up your blackberries, all of which have been gathered prior to this day, as any gathered on Michaelmas Day are spoilt by the devil.

You need approximately;
Half a pound of blackberries,
1 large Bramley apple, peeled, quartered and cored.
A cup of flour (if plain add half tsp of baking powder),1 tablespoon of butter.
Granulated sugar to taste, cold milk, 1 and half cups of water.

Rub the butter and flour until it resembles fine bread crumbs. Stir in the sugar. Stir in about four spoons of milk and mix together to form soft dough which should be divided into four and each piece pressed into a flat circle. Mould the circle of dough around a quarter of apple, to cover it, sealing it shut. Do this for each piece. Place the water in a pan and add a heaped dessert spoon of sugar. Stir until it dissolves and then bring to the boil. Add the blackberries and then place the dumplings on top of them in the pan and cover and simmer for about half an hour. The dumplings should look fluffy. Serve warm with cream or custard. In parts of Scotland there is a custom of baking special bread called Michaelmas Bannock on the eve of the east of Saint Michael's Day. The bread, made from equal parts of barley, oats, and rye with no metal tool being used in its making, were made in remembrance of absent friends or those who had died.

Any animal born on Michaelmas Day was thought to be particularly mischievous. Kittens were called Blackberry Kittens and if tortoise shell were considered very lucky.

Nottingham Goose Fair
First Wednesday in October

Mediaeval fairs were held for a variety of reasons. Sometimes people would offer themselves and their talents up for employment at 'hiring fairs' and sometimes, as in the case of Nottingham, fairs were held so that people could stock up on provisions to last them through the harsh winter season, and these were known as 'goods fairs'. The Goose Fair at Nottingham can be traced back to 1290, when King Edward I granted a charter to allow the town of Nottingham to hold a fair that could last 21 days, beginning on St Edmund's Eve. Some 20,000 geese were walked from the Lincolnshire fens to be sold at the fair and eaten at Michaelmas.

All manner of things came to be sold at the Goose Fair including sheep, cattle, pigs, horses and locally-produced goods such as lace and hosiery. Women were also sold, a practice Thomas Hardy used in his tale, 'The Mayor of Casterbridge'. As time went on, other attractions came to be seen such as dwarves, unicorns, mermaids, fat ladies, bearded ladies, a big wheel, a helter skelter and a roundabout. Today, the fair is visited by thousands of people during the first full weekend of October and is held on the Forest Recreation Ground.

> Snottingham was believed to have been the home of Snot the Wise. Following the Norman Conquest, the name of this town was modified to Nottingham.

Quit Rent Ceremonies
Between 11th October & 11th November

A 'quit rent' was a nominal payment or presentation made to the Lord of the Manor in lieu of customary services and would often take the form of an obligation of some sort.

Each year, a special ceremony takes place on a day between St Michael's Day (11 October) and St Martin's Day (11 November), when the Corporation of the City of London pays two quit rents. For the first rent, the Corporation presents The Queen's Remembrancer with a sharp knife and a blunt knife. A hazel rod, one cubit in length and as thick as the Remembrancer's forefinger, is bent over the blunt knife, leaving a mark which is then cut in two by the sharp knife. This particular ceremony dates back to 1211, and is believed to be linked to the use of tally sticks, where the two halves of a single stick would be given to the two parties to seal a bargain. The role of Remembrancer was created by King Henry II in 1164, and is the oldest judicial post in Britain; his duty was to 'put the King in remembrance of all things owing to the King'. The second quit rent is paid during the same ceremony, and covers the use of a forge located in the delightfully-named Tweezer's, or Twizzer's Alley near The Strand in London. For this, the Corporation presents the Remembrancer with six horseshoes and sixty-one horseshoe nails.

Onion Marmalade

Try making this simple, yet fabulous-tasting onion marmalade, a sure winner on anyone's plate! You will need;

6 large red onions,
7 bay leaves,
3 cups
red wine vinegar,
20 crushed black peppercorns,
3 cups
dark brown muscavado sugar,
3 clean jam jars and some small circles of greaseproof paper.

Finely chop the onions and place into a large heavy saucepan – use one with a lid. Add the red wine vinegar, sugar, bay leaves and crushed peppercorns (30 – 35 grinds of black pepper if using a peppermill) and bring to the boil. Cover and simmer gently until the liquid has evaporated and the onions are translucent (about one and a half hours). While the onions are cooking sterilise three clean 1lb jam jars by placing them in a cold oven and then switch on to gas mark 3, 140c. (Do not put the jam jars into a hot oven otherwise they might explode.) After about 30 mins, carefully remove the jam jars from the oven and leave to cool. Cut out three small circles of greaseproof paper, roughly the same diameter as the inside of the jam jars, and put on one side. When the onions are ready, remove the bay leaves and carefully ladle the mixture into the jam jars, dab on a circle of greaseproof paper and screw the lid on tightly. When completely cool, wipe the sides of the jam jars to remove any spillages and add a label. Store in the fridge, will last 4 – 6 months.

Faerie Rings

Faerie rings are naturally occurring arcs of fungus which can sometimes grow as large as ten metres in diameter. They can establish themselves for many years and become a regular sight, particularly during late autumn in woodland clearings and shady grassy areas. They have long been considered a portal to the faerie realm but, as the old Scottish rhyme suggests, nothing good can come from stepping inside one.

> He wha tills the fairies' green
> Nae luck again shall hae:
> And he wha spills the fairies' ring
> Betide him want and wae.
> For weirdless days and weary nights
> Are his till his deein' day.
> But he wha gaes by the fairy ring,
> Nae dule nor pine shall see,
> And he wha cleans the fairy ring
> An easy death shall dee.

It was believed that rings were formed by faeries and elves dancing; or on the appearance of fey folk in the realm of man. Some believed that a faerie could be caught when returning to the ring. Destroying a faerie ring is both bad luck and pointless as it will only keep growing back until the faeries themselves have decided they are done with it.

The Mirrie Dancers

The Mirrie Dancers is the name given to the Northern Lights in Northern Scotland, Orkney and Shetland. The word 'mirrie', often wrongly thought to be a mispronunciation of merry, in fact means shimmering. The name describes the way the lights move across the sky, as does the folk song 'The Northern Lights of Old Aberdeen':

'She called them the heavenly dancers, merry dancers in the sky'.

Appropriately their Gaelic name is 'Na Fir-Chlis', which is translated as 'the nimble or lively ones'. However, there is a more troubling aspect to their appearance as told in an old Scottish proverb:

'When the mirrie dancers play, they are like to slay'.

Many believed they were the result of fights among sky warriors or fallen angels and that blood from their wounds fell as the bloodstones or heliotropes that can be found in the Hebrides. There is an old story of a young boy who goes out fishing and falls asleep in his boat. When he wakes he sees giants dancing around a great bonfire above his head but then realises they are not dancing but fighting and his boat is adrift on a pool of blood. When he returns to shore he finds he has been gifted with second sight. The red aurora seen during intense solar storms would have been reflected in the lake making it appear as blood.

> **There is a belief that you should not wave, sing or whistle in the presence of the 'Mirrie Dancers' for fear of being whisked away by the spirits that inhabit them.**

SAMHAIN
OCTOBER 31ˢᵗ

Samhain is one of the four main Celtic festivals known as 'quarter days' which fall between the equinoxes and solstices. The meaning of the word Samhain in old Irish is 'summer's end' (from summer, samh and end, fuin). In Ireland 'Oíche Shamnha'(night of Samhain) is when the Aos Sí, who are also known as the 'shining one's' or faeries, come from their mounds accompanied by the dead, this being possible because the veil between worlds is thinnest at this time of the year. People feared being taken by Aos Si and so they would stay indoors and place candles in carved turnips to protect their home. Food and drink would be left outside or a place was set at the dinner table for those now in the 'otherworld' in the hope it would prevent mischief.

All Hallows Eve
31st October

The term 'All Hallows' Eve' is first mentioned in Middle English in The Chronicle of Robert of Gloucester in 1556, although 'All Hallows' is found in earlier Old English manuscripts. The word 'Hallowe'en' means 'Holy' or 'Saints' Evening'. In Scots, the word for 'eve' is 'even', which became contracted to 'e'en' or 'een'.

In the Old Celtic calendar, the year began with the arrival of the darkness at Calan Gaeaf / Samhain, so the last evening before the new month was, in effect, 'old-year's night'. Samhain was the time when the animals were brought down from the high ground to the low fields in readiness for winter and were then walked between bonfires to purify them. It was time for them to be slaughtered to provide food for the months ahead.

Perhaps it is this act which makes us associate this time of year with the dead. It was certainly acknowledged by the early Christian church, which often changed pre-Christian beliefs as little as possible to encourage people's acceptance of Christianity.

This time of year became known as All-Hallowtide or Hollantide and consisted of All Saints' Eve (Hallowe'en), All Saints' Day (otherwise All Hallows or Hallowmas) and All Souls' Day. Its place in the religious calendar was established in the eighth century by Pope Gregory III.

The Tale of Tam Lin and Janet

The Scottish tale of Tam Lin and Janet culminates on 'Oidhche Shamhna' or Samhain (Hallowe'en). Tam Lin was taken by the Fairy Queen after he fell from his horse and she then made him an elven knight, tasked with guarding Carterheugh Forest. Tam Lin later became known for taking the virtue of young women who ventured into the forest.

Despite this, Janet entered the forest and went to the well, where she plucked a rose, causing Tam Lin to appear. Even though Janet was a strong woman, Tam Lin charmed her into 'lying with him', resulting in her pregnancy. Janet later returned to the well to collect some herbs to cause a miscarriage, but met Tam Lin. He told Janet that he was once a mortal and wanted them to bring up their child together.

However, every seven years, on Hallowe'en, the fairies were obliged to give one of their own as a teind (tithe) to Hell and this year it was to be Tam Lin. Janet was determined to save him and Tam Lin told her how to do this. On the appointed night she saw him on his white steed and, as instructed, pulled him from the horse and held him tight. The enraged Queen turned him into all manner of beasts in an attempt to make Janet let go, but she held on. Finally, he was turned into a burning coal, which Janet threw into the well, whereupon Tam Lin reappeared as a man. Janet then hid him with her green cloak and finally won her knight.

The tale of Tam Lin can be dated back to at least as early as 1549, the publication date of The Complaynt of Scotland, which mentions 'The Tayl of the ʒong Tamlene' (The Tale of the Young Tamelene) among a long list of mediaeval romances. The story has many variations in which it has been told, sung or written.

In Carterhaugh Woods near Selkirk there is a water trough through which a well once flowed, called 'Tamlane's Well'. Some people believe this is the well mentioned in the tale of Tam Lin and Janet.

Guy Fawkes' Night
5th November

Guy Fawkes' Night is a residual custom from earlier times when Samhain bonfires and non-Christian ways were frowned upon and even banned in the name of a puritanical observance of Christianity. In 1605, Guy Fawkes together with thirteen other Catholic men sought to destroy Parliament and the protestant King James I. As we know, the plot failed, resulting in the death of most of the plotters. Fawkes is remembered because he was the man who was to ignite the gunpowder and who was tortured into revealing details of the plot.

To celebrate the King's survival people lit bonfires across London. Several months later, 'The Observance of 5th November Act' enforced an annual day of public thanksgiving for the plot's failure, which offended Catholics, especially when effigies of not just Guy Fawkes, but also the Pope, were burnt with much merriment. Also, of course, it allowed the banned Samhain 'end of summer' bonfires to continue as people simply altered the time of their celebrations.

> *'Remember, remember the fifth of November,*
> *Gunpowder, treason and plot.*
> *I see no reason, why gunpowder treason,*
> *should ever be forgot.*
> *Guy Fawkes, Guy Fawkes, 'Twas his intent,*
> *to blow up the king and Parliament.*
> *Three - score barrels of powder below,*
> *Poor old England to overthrow.*
> *By God's providence he was catched,*
> *With a dark lantern and a burning match.'*

The custom of bonfires and fireworks on 5th November has become one of our strongest traditions and every year the rooms beneath Parliament are still checked by the Yeomen of the Guard as a reminder of this early terrorist attack on the state.

Martinmas Sacrifice
11th November

Saint Martin's Day on 11th November was also known as the Funeral of Saint Martin, or Martinmas, as well as Old Hallowe'en and Old Hallowmas Eve.

It became known as a day of sacrifice and blood-letting. In Ireland, on the eve of St. Martin's Day, it was traditional to sacrifice a cockerel by bleeding it. The blood was then collected and sprinkled on the four corners of the house.

Also, no wheel of any kind was to turn on St. Martin's Day because of the death he suffered when he was thrown into a mill stream to be killed by the wheel.

Martlemass beef came from the cattle slaughtered at Martinmas; it was then salted to preserve it for the winter.

The term 'St. Martin's Summer' referred to what people believed was a brief warm spell at the time of St Martin's Day, before the winter months began in earnest.

It is the day of Martinmas
Cups of ale shall freely pass.
What though winter has begun
To push down the summer sun.
To our fire we can betake
And enjoy the crackling brake;
Never heeding winter's face
On the day of Martinmas.

We now know 11th November as Armistice Day. On this day we commemorate the sacrifice and bloodshed of the brave who fell during all wars, but particularly the First and Second World Wars.

Stir Up Sunday
The last Sunday before Advent

'Stir up the pud we beseech thee, the pudding is in the pot, and when we get home we'll eat it all hot'.'

This is one of the many versions of rhymes relating to 'Stir Up Sunday' which is the last Sunday before advent. It was so called because of the 'Stir up, Oh Lord we beseech thee', which was heard by church goers at this time of year and which coincided with making Christmas cakes and puddings. Advent at one time was a time of fasting and so making delicious and tempting food that was to be eaten at Christmas, the end of their fast, had great significance. Rituals such as having the entire household present and each stirring the pudding three times sun-wise were followed, as was placing a silver 'joey', a threepenny bit, into the mixture in the belief that wealth would be bestowed to whoever bit into it on Christmas day as the pudding was eaten. The making of the pudding was only the beginning of its special treatment as on Christmas Day it will be set a flame by brandy being poured over it and carried into the family gathering with much ceremony.

The first of December traditionally marks a 'count-down' to the festive season. In churches special 'advent' candles are lit each Sunday throughout the season, a tradition that was taken into the home through single candles with markers for each day being burnt leading up to Christmas Eve. For many the custom of opening 'doors' on Advent calendars are a fun way of building up the excitement of the coming holiday period.

The Wren (Troglodytes troglodytes) & The Robin (Erithacus rubecula)

British and Irish folklore often join these two birds together as sweethearts, the robin being the male and (Jenny) wren being the female. Both were believed to possess magical qualities and so to kill either would bring bad luck. However the St Stephen's Day practice of wren hunting ignored the superstition and this poor, tiny, innocent bird was hunted and killed for sport. The origins of why are unclear. The wren was associated with the Celts and Druids and they called it the 'magus' bird' meaning its actions were omens of the future. One possible explanation is that it represented the killing of 'pagan ways'.

Both the wren and robin were meant to have pitied the dead. There are many stories of them covering any dead creatures they came upon with moss and other woodland materials. These kind gestures gave them a reputation for being compassionate. Their association with the yuletide season is in part due to them being very active and frequently seen in winter when other birds are less active or have migrated.

Eggnog

Eggnog is believed to have originated from East Anglia. Its recipe may have developed from a 'posset' which is a mediaeval beverage made from warm milk. 'Nog' may stem from the word 'noggin' which is a Middle, possibly Norfolk dialect term for a wooden vessel used to serve alcohol. It was also known as Egg Flip because of the 'flipping' action, or 'rapid pouring' of the mixture between two containers required to mix it.

4 egg yolks
½ cup Demerara sugar
2 cups milk pinch cinnamon
1 tsp vanilla extract or split vanilla pod
1 cup cream
1 cup Madeira, rum or whisky
½ cup brandy
1 tsp freshly grated nutmeg

In a large bowl, whisk the egg yolks until they become lighter in colour. Slowly add the sugar, beating after each addition and whisking until fluffy. Combine the milk, cinnamon and vanilla in a thick-bottomed saucepan and then heat slowly until the milk mixture is quite hot, but not boiling. Next, whisking all the time to prevent the mixture splitting, carefully add the hot milk mixture to the eggs. Return the mixture to the saucepan and heat gently, stirring constantly until the mixture begins to thicken slightly and coats the back of a wooden spoon. Do not allow the mixture to boil.

Remove from the heat and stir in the cream and alcohol and sprinkle with a little nutmeg. Finally, pour into some pretty cups and serve either warm or chilled. If you have a vegan in the house, substitute coconut milk and use rum for an excellent alternative. It can also be made without alcohol for a more traditional 'posset' taste. All that remains is to toast happiness and enjoy!

Holly & Ivy

An old song named by some as 'The battle of Holly and Ivy' and possibly a precursor to the more traditional carol 'The Holly and the Ivy' reflects the battle of light and dark witnessed at the Solstice and the tradition of evergreens being a symbol of hope throughout this barren season.

Holly stands in the hall, fair to behold:
Ivy stands without the door, she is full sore a cold.
Nay, ivy, nay, it shall not be I wis;
Let holly have the mastery, as the manner is.
Holly and his merry men, they dance and they sing,
Ivy and her maidens, they weep and they wring.
Nay, ivy, nay, it shall not be I wis;
Let holly have the mastery, as the manner is
Ivy hath chapped fingers, she caught them from the cold,
So might they all have, aye, that with ivy hold.
Nay, ivy, nay, it shall not be I wis;
Let holly have the mastery, as the manner is.
Holly hath berries red as any rose,
The forester, the hunter, keep them from the does.
Nay, ivy, nay, it shall not be I wis;
Let holly have the mastery, as the manner is.
Ivy hath berries black as any sloe;
There come the owl and eat him as she go.
Nay, ivy, nay, it shall not be I wis;
Let holly have the mastery, as the manner is.
Holly hath birds a fair full flock,
The nightingale, the popinjay, the gentle laverock.
Nay, ivy, nay, it shall not be I wis;
Let holly have the mastery, as the manner is.
Goodivy, what birds hast thou?
None but the owlet that cries how, how.
Nay, ivy, nay, it shall not be I wis;
Let holly have the mastery, as the manner is.

Winter

Now is the time for evergreens to shine as ivy berries provide a last sticky feast for insects on weak sunlit days. Not only do holly berries and mistletoe give us excellent yuletide decorations but also provide food to birds such as the winter visiting mistle thrush, who inadvertently carries the seed from the mistletoe to other trees where it might thrive as a beautiful parasite.

An old Elizabethan carol which may well be a precursor of the well-known 'The Holly and the Ivy' has a verse 'Holly hath berries as red as any Rose, The Forrester and Hunter keep them for the Does, Ivy has berries as black as any Sloes; Then comes the Owl and eats them as she Goes'. Whilst the facts may not accurate regarding the owl's propensity to eat ivy berries it reminds us of the importance these plants play when little else grows.

Cool and calm winter nights are an excellent time to take starlit walks; often accompanied by an owl that you will certainly hear and now stand a better chance of seeing, as there is little cover close to its favourite perching posts. 'Moss buttons' form a velvety green padded quilt under trees and are just one of the many mosses that thrive in our damp climate however moss is known as 'charcoal burner' as it likes to grow on burnt ground given the chance.

WINTER SOLSTICE
21ST or 22ND DECEMBER

In the British Isles our history has meant we have a mix of cultural and religious celebration. In a more pagan tradition people will be celebrating the Goddess once again becoming the Great Mother and giving birth to the new Sun King, or for others it is the time of the Crone, the Holly Lord, The Oak Lord and Herne the Hunter escort to the Goddess. In a Christian tradition it is the birth of the Christ Child. As we become a more culturally diverse society new celebrations will meld into old ones. Traditionally this time of the year would have been marked by bonfires bringing light and warmth to the dark cold days of winter. Whatever your beliefs whether religious, nature based or if you choose no belief there is one thing we all have in common, that this time of the year feels 'special' and is a time to be marked.

A Staffordshire Christmas

Charles Poole bemoaned the changes in celebrating Christmas in his book Customs, Superstitions and Legends of the County of Stafford in 1875.

'The season of the Nativity is now no longer marked by that hospitality which characterised its observance among our forefathers. In many an ancient hall of the shire, the Squire would assemble all his tenants and neighbours at day break. The strongest beer was broached, and the horns went plentifully about with toast, sugar, nutmeg, and good Cheshire cheese. Every one ate heartily, and everyone was welcome. The wassail-bowl, the yule-log, the Lord of Misrule, together with many other customs of ancient days made our 'Merrie Englande' conspicuous among the nations of Europe for its observance of Christmastide; the decking of churches and houses with holly and other evergreens, and invitations to family parties, together with the issue of so-called Christmas numbers (advent calendar) published months before the blessed festival dawns, and, sad to say, having scarcely any illusion to it, are the only reminders of this glorious season'.

The favourite wassail drink of Staffordshire & the Black Country was said to be elderberry wine rather than ale.

A popular wassail was;

*'A jolly Wassel bowl,
A wasell of good ale.
Well fare the butler's soul
That setteth this on sale,
Our jolly wassell!'*

Midnight on Christmas Eve

Christmas Eve and particularly midnight on this day warrants more superstitions than Christmas day itself. In Lancashire, Cheshire and Nottinghamshire it is believed the bells of long fallen and buried churches ring out of midnight, that Rosemary burst into flower (Gloucestershire and Berkshire), faeries would meet at the bottom of mines and say a mass to celebrate the Christ Child's birth (Black Country), that doors and windows should be opened to let out bad spirits, that farm animals kneeled, that farm animals could talk and that bees hum the hundredth psalm.

Throughout the day and evening people were worried about evil spirits roaming before they were banished on Christmas Day so much so that in the Midlands some would wear a sprig of mistletoe about their neck to protect them against witchcraft. It was considered very unlucky to cut the Yule cake before this day and that it was unlucky to give out a light from a Christmas Eve fire.

Divination was also practised on this day. If a girl walked backwards to a pear tree and then walked round it three times she would see a vision of her future husband or if she went into the garden and picked twelve sage leaves she would see the shadowy form of her future husband (Northamptonshire).

> *'My song save this, is little worth*
> *I lay my weary pen aside,*
> *And wish you health, and love, and mirth,*
> *As fits solemn Christmas tide,*
> *Be this, good friends, our carol still*
> *Be peace on earth, be peace on earth,*
> *To all of gentle will.'*

Yuletide Snippets

It is said that King Arthur was the first person to celebrate Christmas in AD521 in the city of York. Prior to this the 25th December was dedicated to Satan, or to heathen deities. Arthur took up his winter quarters at York and held a festival of Christmastide

Boxing Day gets its name from the practice of opening boxes that contained money given to those who had given their service during the year. It was also the day when alms boxes, placed in churches on Christmas Day, were opened to help the poor and needy.

Victorian high society marked New Year's Day by holding open houses for their unmarried daughters to meet local eligible bachelors. The bachelor would most likely receive invitations from a number of households and would spend a short time in each chatting with the potential suitor before moving on to his next engagement.

Twelfth Night
5th or 6th January

Twelfth Night was a time for many strange customs. One of the more unusual ones is the annual contest of the Haxey Hood which takes place in the village of Haxey in North Lincolnshire. Villagers try to get a leather tube called a 'hood' into one of four pubs in Haxey or the nearby village of Westwoodside. It consists of 'tackles and shoving' between villagers in a tradition that can take many hours to complete. Its origins date back to the 14th century, when Lady de Mowbray's silk riding hood was blown away by the wind and farm workers chased it until it was caught. The man who retrieved it was said too be too shy to hand it back to the Lady, so he passed it to one of the others to hand back. The Lady thanked the man who returned the hood saying he had acted like a Lord, whereas the man who had actually caught the hood was a Fool. For this act of chivalry and the chase which had amused her she donated thirteen acres of land on condition that the chase should be re-enacted each year.

In Leominster, Shropshire, Morris men and mummers parade from The Boot Inn, Oreleton, to the local orchards to wassail the trees to ensure a bountiful crop of cider apples for the year ahead. This custom involves lighting torches, dancing, singing and placing a piece of Christmas cake soaked in cider on the branches of an apple tree and sprinkling cider around the tree's roots. Following the ceremony, mummers perform a traditional play based on the legend of St George.

Plough Monday- Back to Work Day!

In theory it was back to work on the first Monday after the Epiphany/Twelfth Night. However it would have been a slow start as the day was marked by customs and frivolity. The young plough boys known as 'bullocks', 'jacks' or 'stots' would be in their freshly laundered white shirts and decorated in ribbons and rosettes, brasses and bells and were then tied to the plough which was taken around the village. Often this was accompanied by Sword and Morris dancers with fiddles, pipes and accordion. Pennies were collected along the route.

Plough Plays akin to mumming were popular and in Revesby, Lincolnshire a script from 1779 lists a cast of Pickle Herring, Blue Breeches, Christmas Mumming and Ginger Breeches. In Goathland, near Whitby the dancing was begun with clashes of swords and followed patterns that were thought to have been brought to these shores by the invading Norsemen over a thousand years ago. In parts of east England a 'straw bear' (a man covered in straw) was led by a leash around the inns, singing and dancing.

It was the day when newcomers were initiated to the craft of leading horses and ploughing. In Cambridgeshire a boy's nose would be rubbed in the horse's vent as a means of welcoming him to the team.

The Eve of St. Agnes
20th January

St. Agnes, the patron Saint of engaged couples, has attracted many stories and the eve of her anniversary is associated with divination associated with virtue and matrimony. She was asked to abandon her Christian God to worship Roman deities, but she refused. It is said she was sent to prison among 'persons of ill-fame', but she maintained her virtue; she was then thrown into a burning fire, from which she came unhurt; she was finally beheaded January on 21st AD 304. There are many wells, churches and springs dedicated to her and it is said that a visit by lovers to such a place on the eve of her death will mean they see their future.

'They told her how, upon St. Agnes' Eve,
Young virgins might have visions of delight,
And soft adorings from their loves receive,
Upon the honey'd middle of the night,
If ceremonies due they did aright;
As, supperless to bed they must retire,
And couch supine their beauties, lily white;
Nor look behind, nor sideways, but require
Of Heaven with upward eyes for all that they desire'.

(extract) by John Keats

Mistle Thrush (Turdus viscivorus)

The Mistle Thrush is a bird of many names: Mizzly Dick, Jeremy Joy, Butcher Bird, Big Mavis, Mistles and Bull Thrush. Its Linnaean name Turdus viscivorus reveals it to be a 'devourer of mistletoe'. According to folklore it is believed to be deaf, to speak seven languages and to grow a new set of legs every decade.

As Britain's largest songbird, the Mistle Thrush can be seen throughout the cold months in open parkland, orchards and suburban gardens. At eleven inches long, it is noticeably larger than its much commoner cousin, the Song Thrush, but has an overall paler appearance, ash-brown upper parts, a buff breast, heavily marked with chestnut wedges and white flashes to its underwing. An alert and spirited bird, its dry, clattering alarm call has been compared to wood being scraped against a comb and gives rise to local nicknames such as Skrite, Jercock and Holm Screech. A Renaissance poem: 'The Harmony of Birds', describes its carolling as 'Sanctus, Sanctus'.

English folk belief maintains that the mistletoe's viscous fruits can only germinate once they have passed through a thrush's system. The plant's name derives from an ancient word for 'dung twig' but is just as likely to refer to the wiping of sticky beaks on branches!

Jack Frost

In these days of central heating, our houses rarely seem to be visited by Jack Frost. This spirit of the winter is believed to be a variant of Old Man Winter. He is thought of as a mischievous sprite who drapes the landscape overnight with cold silvery white crystals, creates crispy icy tips on leaves and paints wonderful swirls and fernlike patterns on our windows. His icy grip is to be avoided, as we are warned that he will nip at our extremities – especially our nose, fingers and toes!

His origins may stem from an Anglo-Saxon and Nordic folklore figure called Jokul Frosti. In Scotland, during the winter months, a female called Cailleach Bheur, or Winter Hag, walks the Highlands bearing a holly staff with a crow perched upon her shoulder. Images of Jack Frost, particularly Victorian prints and cards, often depict him with a paint brush in his hand demonstrating the artistry of this mythological creature who belongs as much to the faerie realm as to that of man.

Grey Peas and Bacon

Grey peas (pronounced pays) and bacon bits was a 'poor man's meal' strongly associated with the Black Country, in the West Midlands, England. It is closely related to the mediaeval peasant's dish of pease pottage or pease pudding. Many pubs in the local area still serve the meal with a bread cob. The traditional brown peas used for the dish were also used as pigeon food and it was not unusual for people to buy their peas from the local pet shop. It is now made using Carlin Peas. The recipe below suggests the meal was not confined to the Black Country originally as it was in a nationwide cookbook but it appears for some reason has stuck with the area.

For gray pese. Fyrst stepe thy pese over the nyet, And trendel hom clene, and fayre hom dyet. Sethe hom in water; and brothe thou take Of bacun, and fresshe bre thou nowt forsake; Summe men hom lofe alyed wyle With floure and summe with never a dele; these pese with bacun eten may be As tho whyet pese were, so mot I the. But tho white with powder of peper tho Moun be forsyd with ale there to.

Original Recipe in the verse cookery book 'Liber Cure Cocorum', 1430

CURIOS of the BRITISH ISLES

In this final chapter I have looked through the past ten years of the Country Wisdom and Folklore Diaries and picked out some of the interesting people and places we have discovered in our travels, from Long Meg and her Daughters in Cumbria to the last surviving Ducking Stool which can be found in Leominster Priory in Herefordshire,

These little anecdotes do not fit into any part of the Wheel of the Year, but they are never the less very interesting and deserve a mention in any journey through the folklore of the British Isles.

Long Meg & her Daughters, Cumbria

'Long Meg and her daughters' is a 350ft diameter stone circle situated in Little Salkeld, Cumbria. Long Meg herself is a 12ft high monolith with three symbols and four corners that face towards the points of the compass; she stands outside the circle of her daughters. It is supposedly impossible to count how many stones there are because of trickery still within the site.

According to legend, the circle's origin comes from the story of a wizard called Michael Scott who saw a witches' sabbath taking place and turned all the participants to stone. Some believe there is treasure buried beneath Long Meg and others tell of Long Meg bleeding if she is chipped. In the late 18th century Colonel Lacey attempted to blow up the circle but was stopped by a severe storm. The stones date from approximately 1500 BC, Long Meg is local red sandstone and her daughters are rhyolite, a form of granite.

Ducking Stool

Leominster is believed to be the last place in England where the ducking stool was used. In 1817 Sarah Leeke was wheeled around the town in the device, but was spared ducking because the river was considered too low. You can still see this ducking stool in the Priory Church at Leominster which has, in recent times held a service of penitence for both the historical injustice meted out by this instrument of torture, but also present day intolerance and prejudice.

In 1378 Piers Plowman refers to the cucking stool, cucking meaning scold in Saxon, as a form of 'wyuen pine', meaning women's punishment. It later became known as the ducking stool and was an instrument of humiliation and torture most commonly, though not exclusively, for women.

It became mandatory for manors to have these devices and to keep them in good working order as a means of punishing people for minor offences. It was in fact a chair, rather than a stool. The person was shackled to it, and then the chair was raised in the air by the long arm attached to the chair. This was then wheeled around the town so all could see the perpetrator of some offence such as gossiping, prostitution, practising witchcraft, cuckolding or illicit trade practices. The arm would then be swung over water and the victim would be plunged into it.

Cunning Folk

It is thought that in mediaeval times there were many thousands of Cunning Folk across the British Isles. This name was one of many used to describe people who used folk magic as a means of making a living or supplementing their income. 'Let me see how many trades have I to live by: First, I am a wise-woman, and a fortune-teller, and under that I deal in physicke and fore-speaking, in palmistry, and recovering of things lost. Next, I undertake to cure madd folkes; then I keepe gentlewomen lodgers, to furnish such chambers as I let out by the night: Then I am provided for bringing young wenches to bed; and, for a need, you see I can play the match-maker.' Thomas Heywood's 1638 play, 'The Wise Woman of Hogsdon.'

Most Cunning Folk were Christians who saw themselves as selling a service that could help others and they often used the Bible as a source for their craft. Their services were commonly sought for opposing witchcraft, healing, locating criminals and property and assisting in love magic. The 'knowledge' they had was often passed through generations of one family and many kept a grimoire, a book in which instructions for charms, spells and procedures were written down and added to by each family practitioner.

Wyrms

Worm Hill in County Durham is said to bear the scars of a great worm, known as the Lambton Worm, which coiled itself around the hill and terrorised the region during medieval times.

It was named after John Lambton, heir to the Lambton estate in County Durham, who on going fishing rather than attending church one Sunday pulled out a strange eel-like creature with the head of a salamander and nine holes on either side of its skull. He then threw it down a well. Years passed and John Lambton went to fight in the Crusades. Meanwhile the creature thrived and grew inside the well, poisoning the water, before finally emerging and terrorizing the village. When John returned and saw the destruction, he consulted a witch, who told him to have his armour covered in razor-sharp spear points and to fight the worm in the river. This he did, protected by his armour, he saw the parts of the worm being swept away by the river as he sliced at it in victory.

However the witch had warned him that, after his victory he must kill the first living thing he saw or the Lambton family would be cursed for nine generations with no heir dying peacefully in his bed. Unfortunately, because his father forgot to release a hound for John to kill, he became the first living thing John saw. Feeling unable to kill his father, he brought the curse upon his family.

Apotropaic Marks

Apotropaic marks, also known as witch marks, are symbols or patterns scratched into the fabric of a building to protect against witches. Apotropaic comes from the Greek 'apotrepein' –'apo' meaning away and 'trepein' meaning to turn. Through this type of counter-magick, evil was thought to be kept at bay and such symbols have been used to make amulets and talismans, particularly as a protection against the evil eye.

Carvings have been found at Shakespeare's Birthplace in Stratford-upon-Avon, at the Tower of London and on many churches as well as everyday buildings. The marks are most commonly found near places where witches were thought to be able to enter such as doors, windows or chimneys. They take many forms such as: a flower-like pattern of overlapping circles, the intertwined letters V and M or a double V (for the Virgin Mary or Virgo Virginum), crisscrossing lines that were meant to confuse any spirits that might try to follow them and a dot within a circle signifying a mirror to the evil eye.

The Pittenweem Witches

Pittenweem, a fishing village in Fife, was the scene of terrible brutality in 1704. Beatrix Laing asked Patrick Morton, the blacksmith's son, to forge her some nails but was told he was too busy so she went away muttering evil under her breath. She was later seen throwing hot embers into cold water by the boy, who became convinced he was bewitched.

Reverend Cowper persuaded Patrick to say that Beatrix Laing had cast spells on him and he also named Isobel Adam, Janet Cornfoot and Mistress Lawson, together with several other villagers. As a result they were held in the local gaol. The minister ordered the prisoners be subjected to degradation and torture. Beatrix Laing was forced to stay awake for five days and nights before she confessed to being a witch. She was beaten, held in stocks and thrown into the 'thieves' hole' where she spent five months in solitary confinement. The remaining prisoners were brutally tortured until they confessed. When enlightened villagers pleaded for mercy to be shown it was agreed that Beatrix Laing and the others should be fined the sum of five shillings and set free. However Beatrix was chased by a mob from the village and she later died of her injuries.

The story continued for poor, Janet Cornfoot, who was dragged to the beach, a rope was twisted around her waist with one end attached to a ship lying offshore and the other end held by a gang of men. She was swung into the sea until she was almost drowned and then dragged onto the sand to be beaten. A heavy wooden door was placed atop of her and boulders heaped on it until she was crushed. A horse and sledge passed over her several times. Her remains were refused a Christian burial. No action was ever taken against her killers, even though Patrick Morton later confessed that his accusations had been totally false.

Bowerman's Nose

Bowerman's Nose is a tall column of granite rock on Dartmoor that has a story to tell of a hunter called Bowerman, who was a well-liked, jovial man who lived on the moor. At that time Dartmoor was plagued by witches who met in the secluded moorland and made villagers fearful. Bowerman, who travelled the moors with his pack of hounds, was not frightened of the witches and encouraged the villagers to feel the same, thereby taking away the witches power.

One dark autumn evening Bowerman's pack got the scent of a hare which turned into a narrow valley. On making chase he came upon a coven of witches. The hare, followed by the pack and hunter ran through the gathering and enraged the witches. In revenge a witch named Levera changed her shape into a hare and enticed Bowerman and his pack into hours of chase. When the hounds and huntsman were exhausted she led them to an ambush of shrieking witches who cast a powerful spell, turning Bowerman and his hounds to stone where they stood. You can still see the stone figure that was once Bowerman and his pack at the site of Bowerman's Nose and on a moonless night you can hear them chasing their quarry.

> *A postscript to the story of Bowerman is that the people of Dartmoor were so enraged when they heard about the fate of their friend that they determined to drive the witches out of Devon. The witches took to their broomsticks and were carried on the wind over the Bristol Channel into Wales. It is said in Devon that this is why many women in Wales wore tall, pointed hats.*

The Ballad of the Bloody Miller

The Ballad of The Bloody Miller was a popular song based on a true crime committed in 1684 in Hogstow, near Minsterley in Shropshire. It tells the sad tale of Anne Nichols, who became pregnant by the miller's servant, Francis Cooper, with whom she had been in a relationship. On hearing Anne was expecting a child and being urged by her father to marry her, Cooper 'most wickedly and barbarously murder(ed) her'. The ballad, which was mass produced as a broadsheet, now remains as a lone surviving copy among the Pepys Ballads at Magdalene College, Cambridge.

Evidence that this crime actually happened comes from an entry in the diary of a puritan clergyman, Philip Henry, on 20 February of that year: *'I heard of a murther near Salop on Sabb. day ye 10, a woman fathering a conception on a Milner was Kild by him in a feild, her Body lay there many dayes by reason of ye Coroner's absence'*.

The Bloody Miller's victim begs for her life in this illustration from Samuel Pepys' copy, which dates back to about 1685.

In addition, the burial is recorded on 1 March of 'Anne Nicholas, truculenter occisa', that is, violently murdered (the surname is considered close enough). The delayed burial, following her murder on 10 February, fits in with Philip Henry's diary entry about a delay due to the absence of the coroner. Also recorded is the baptism on 24 March of Ichabod, son of Francis Cooper, 'homicide' (i.e. murderer), thought to be his illegitimate son from an affair with another woman, to which the lover confesses in the ballad. As for Francis Cooper, he would have been incarcerated, put on trial executed and buried in an unmarked grave.

Stiperstones

Geologists believe the Stiperstones, a rocky ridge in Shropshire, were formed 480 million years ago. They consist of six distinctive rocky outcrops, each with its own name; from north to south these are Shepherd's Rock, Devil's Chair, Manstone Rock, Cranberry Rock, Nipstone Rock and The Rock. There are a number of superstitions associated with the Stiperstones and many folk stories about how they were formed.

One story tells of a curse on the land, which had been so badly ravaged by wars, floods and droughts that it became uninhabitable. The Devil was walking across Salop (the old name for Shropshire) and decided to build his castle in this ungodly area and benefit from its bitter cold climate as a respite from Hell. So he asked six giantesses from Wales to carry stones in their aprons and build his fortress. But a young lord, called Shrobe, saw the giantesses approaching and decided to stop them performing their task. He tripped the first one up with his rope, making her drop 'The Rock'; then he lured the second into a stream and drugged the third with sweet berries. One-by-one they were all tricked into abandoning their loads.
When the Devil returned to view his new castle, he found only six great piles of rock. In his anger, tears of molten lead fell from his eyes and burned into the ground. It was these seams of tears which were mined in later years, from Roman times to 1922.

Sir Francis Drake

There are several traditions extant in connection to Sir Francis Drake, the great naval admiral. Of the supply of water to Plymouth the following legend is given. The laundresses were so distressed for water that they were obliged to send their clothes to Plympton to be washed. Sir Francis rode off in haste to the forest of Dartmoor, and after searching some time he discovered a fine clear spring. He then urged his horse on and galloped into Plymouth, the stream following all the way into the town. (The water supply into Plymouth known as Drakes Leat was taken over by South West Water in 1973 is still in use today)

'Drake was long held to be a magician though only practicing Magia Alba or white magic; many strange tales are recorded concerning him. We hear one day when he was playing skittles on Plymouth Hoe, a messenger informed him of a foreign fleet sailing into harbour, Sir Francis, apparently heeded not the news, but quietly finished his game. He then ordered a large block of timber and a hatchet to be brought to him. He chopped up the wood into little blocks, and then cast them into the sea. At his command each little block became a mighty man-of-war; and within a short time the irresistible strength of these ships proved too overwhelming for the foreign fleet and thus the foes of Queen Elizabeth were totally destroyed'.

From Bygone Days in Devon and Cornwall by Mrs H.P.Whitcome 1874.

Black Tom of Bedford

Black Tom, so named because of his shock of black hair, was a highway man who thieved travellers in and around Bedford in the late 18th century. He was eventually caught, tried and sentenced to death by hanging which took place on the junction of Tavistock Street, Union Street and Clapham Road in Bedford and was buried nearby. He is said to have had a stake driven through his heart to prevent him from rising again as many feared he would. However, this did not work, as a ghost of a man, staggering around with a broken neck, has been seen by many people. In the 1960's witnesses saw a gruesome figure in broad daylight staggering down the road his head lolling as if his neck were broken and claim he just vanished into thin air. Another report from the 1980's of an apparition, who was thought to be an intruder, appearing in a bedroom. Both the man and woman of the residence saw a man in a black cloak with a floppy hat move through the room and then vanish.

It is said that Black Tom's case was cited as a reason for reform in 1775, when John Howard campaigned for the abolition of the 'jailer's fee', paid by prisoners to the jailer for 'upkeep' and release. Black Tom, like many were hanged because they couldn't afford to bribe the jailer to petition for them to the judge, which was likely to have given them a better outcome.

Double Sunset

The town of Leek in Staffordshire became known for the unusual phenomenon of a 'double sunset' at the Summer Solstice. This rare astro-geographical event occurs when the sun appears to set twice on the same evening. The sun appears to set the first time when it drops behind a hill obstructing the horizon line then moments later it emerges from behind the hill and sets for a second time when it drops below the true horizon. The sunset at Leek on the Summer Solstice was first recorded in 1686, by Dr Robert Plot, in his book 'The Natural History of Staffordshire'. The traditional site for observing this particular double sunset was the churchyard of Saint Edward the Confessor, from where the sun appeared to set on the summit of a millstone grit hill, known as The Cloud, situated six miles to the north-west. It then partially reappeared from The Cloud's steep northern slope before setting for a second and final time on the horizon. The last reliable witnessing of this event was filmed from the churchyard in 1977, but sadly, it is no longer visible from this location as trees now obscure the view. However, it may still be observed from the road to Pickwood Hall, off Milltown Way and from Lowe Hill on the outskirts of the town.

West Derbyshire also has sites where a double sunset occurs at the Summer Soltice: Chrome Hill (observed from Glutton Bridge); Parkhouse Hill (observed from Glutton Grange in late March, early April and September) and Thorpe Cloud (from the top of nearby Lin Dale).

Country Wisdom & Folklore Almanac

The Great Orme Goats

For over one hundred years, white Kashmiri goats have been seen scrambling over the Great Orme in Llandudno. Their ancestry can be traced back to two goats acquired by Squire Christopher Tower, from Weald Park, Brentwood in Essex, in an attempt to create a profitable woollen industry. The goats flourished and eventually the squire was able to manufacture a cashmere shawl. King George IV accepted a gift of pair of goats from this herd and established the Windsor herd. Later, two of the Windsor goats were taken to Gloddaeth Hall, near Llandudno, but were later released onto the Great Orme where they were allowed to roam free.

Goats have always been associated with the devil, however they were also thought to bring good luck, especially to farmers. It is still believed by many that if a goat is put with cattle, the cows will not abort. In the same way, if a goat is allowed to run with the flock, the sheep will remain disease-free. Goats are also believed to be able to foresee changes in the weather, as a herd will move up hill before good weather and lower down when they sense a change for the worse. People in Llandudno certainly have good reason to believe goats can predict the weather. In June 1993, many people commented the unusual presence of a large group of billy goats on the land near the old Great Orme Post Office, just prior to the heaviest rainfall ever recorded over Llandudno, which resulted in very serious flooding.

During the great virus of 2020, the Great Orme goats departed the headland and were able to wander the abandoned streets of LLandudno due to the lack of visitors to the town.

Beeston Castle, Cheshire

This particular castle was built as a bastion of power for Earl Ranulf of Chester. The land upon which the castle is built was gifted to the Earl as a reward for his loyal service to the King during the crusades. The castle, built on a sandstone crag, has a design allegedly inspired by the fortresses and castles that the Earl encountered during his military career. Unusually, it has no discernible keep—instead, it has sizeable outer and inner baileys. In addition to its unique design, the inner bailey of the castle was further fortified with a nine metre deep inner ditch—an additional line of defence, common within crusade fortresses in Eastern Europe.

The castle was destroyed by Cromwell's forces in 1646, leaving the ruins we see today. Legend speaks of buried treasure left by Royalists or by King Richard II, who is said to have hidden gold there to keep it from Bollingbroke. Some say the treasure is down the well and guarded by demons; anyone going down the well to retrieve it would be struck dumb or go mad. Another tale associated with the castle is that one day it will save England, although it is not known how or why.

Wolerton Hall

Norfolk In 1727, Horatio Walpole built Wolerton Hall, which later became home to the ghost of 'The White Lady'. She is said to appear at times of calamity or threat to the family and is believed to be one of the Scambler family, who lived in a building on the site, prior to the present hall being built. She was regularly seen by members of the family and their servants. In an attempt to appease her spirit, members of the Walpole family who died would be driven three times around the ruined church in a hearse, before finally being laid to rest in the family vault.

The hall is also haunted by another ghost—the wife of Ambassador Lord Horace Walpole. According to legend, a portrait depicting the lady's husband, together with seven or eight of their children (some of whom were represented as angels, having died as babies), once hung in the drawing room of the hall. Many years later, one of Lord Walpole's descendants cut the painting into segments and distributed the individual portraits of the children amongst other members of the family. This act caused the ambassador's wife to return in spirit, endlessly roaming the house, fruitlessly searching for her lost children.

Source of the Severn

Rivers feature heavily in folklore and mythology. The source of a river is a magickal place where the energy and path begin to create something that can give both life and destruction. On the edges of the Hafren Forest in the uplands of Ptynlimon, the highest massif in the Cambrian Mountains, is the humble beginning of the river we now know as the Severn. It was known to the Romans as Sabrina (after a water spirit). Celtic mythology tells of Sabrina being one of three water nymph sisters who met on Plynlimon (Anglicised name for Pumlumon—the Welsh for Five Peaks) to find their way to the sea. Each sister took a different route; Ystwyth to the west and Varga (the Wye) to the south. Sabrina (the Severn), who loved the land, chose a meandering route that led her to the East. The Celts believed that where two realms met (the forest and river) was particularly magickal. The Severn Way is a 210-mile footpath that traces the course of the river from its source to its mouth in the estuary of Bristol Channel. The River Severn is the longest river in the United Kingdom, being 220 miles long and flowing through the three English counties of Shropshire, Worcestershire and Gloucestershire.

Other tales tell of Sabrina as the daughter of King Locrinus and his mistress Estrildis, a Germanic princess. The king's wife Queen Guendolen, ordered that both Sabrina and her mother be drowned in the river, which was named Sabrina so that Locrinus' betrayal would never be never forgotten.

The Lost Land of Tyno Helig, Conwy

According to legend, the remains of the lost lands of Tyno Helig, an area of land wiped from the face of the earth in retribution for a heinous crime, lie beneath the waters of Conwy Bay. This tragic tale begins when Gwendud, the daughter of a prince, told her suitor, Tathal, that she could not marry him because he did not wear the golden torque (collar) of a nobleman. Desolate, the young man decided to leave and go north to seek his fortune. Soon he came across a Scottish chieftain trying to get home but, instead of helping him, he cruelly murdered him and stole his golden torque. Tathal returned home full of the tale of how he had been set upon by robbers but had managed to kill the leader, who had turned out to be an outlawed nobleman. Overjoyed, Gwendud agreed to marry him.

During the marriage feast, the ghost of the murdered Scottish chieftain appeared and placed a curse upon the family. Nothing happened for many years and the family grew complacent. However, one night when they were celebrating the birth of their great-great-grandchild, one of the servants went to the cellars to get more wine and found them awash with sea water and fish. Instead of raising the alarm, she chose to run away with her lover. Soon the palace, the people and the lands became lost to the sea forever.

St Just in Roseland, Cornwall

The tiny church of St Just in Roseland, built on the former site of a 5th century Celtic chapel, is home to a most curious legend. According to local folklore, this is where Joseph of Arimathaea and his nephew, Jesus, made land when they visited England. It is widely believed that Joseph of Arimithaea was a wealthy trader with strong connections to Cornish tin mines and Somerset lead mines. Many people think he may have brought Jesus with him to meet the Druids on one of his business trips.

William Blake wrote about this legend in his famous poem, 'Jerusalem'. This was set to music by Hubert Parry during the sad and desperate times of the First World War to help promote patriotic feeling. Since that time, this unofficial anthem has become one of the nation's favourites and is sung at gatherings as diverse as rugby matches and Women's Institute meetings.

Whether or not the legend is true, the combination of the water's edge and the wonderful tropical plants and flowers which surround this tiny church makes this a stunningly beautiful place to visit.

Sea Witches

The sea witch has featured in British folklore over the centuries particularly in fishing communities, where sailors still follow rituals and observe superstitions to this day. She can control the natural forces of the weather and the sea, thereby holding the fate of seafarers in her power. The sea witch would sell sailors control of the wind by tying three knots in a rope which, when done in a magickal way bound the wind within. She then told the sailors that pulling the first knot would yield a south-easterly gentle wind, pulling two knots would give a strong northerly wind and three knots a tempest. Often solitary, the sea witch would use moon magick, as the moon controls the tides.

Sir Francis Drake is said to have sold his soul to the devil in order to become a skilled seaman and admiral. So the devil sent him sea witches, who raised a storm that helped him to defeat the Spanish Armada in 1588. The battle occurred near Devil's Point, overlooking Devonport, a place which some people still believe is haunted by witches.

Another tale tells of a sea witch named Morgana who lured sailors to their deaths. After falling in love with a young seaman who was lost to the sea, she vowed to help sailors in their travels. This caused her to become an outcast amongst her sister witches. After trying to help a son of Ares she was impaled with a spear and dissolved into the sea foam—her final resting place.

The Grimes Graves Goddess

Grimes Graves in Norfolk is the remains of a Neolithic flint mine worked between 2200 and 2500 BC. Its name originates from the Anglo Saxons, who believed that it was a mine worked by the god Grim. The numerous grassy hollows mark the existence of over 350 former mine shafts.

During excavations in the late 1930s, archaeologist A L Armstrong made a remarkable discovery. At the end of what appeared to be a short, unproductive gallery, he discovered an altar. In front of the altar he found a naively-carved chalk goddess figure: a lopsided figure with eyes, nose and a mouth, lumpy breasts and two crude arms resting on a protuberant belly. Close to the goddess were several antler picks, a small chalk cup, a chalk phallus and some chalk balls. Two theories exist relating to her existence: the first, that she was an offering to ensure the continued 'fertility' of the mine; and the second, that she was a fake produced to trick Armstrong and his colleagues.

Visiting this ancient site is strongly recommended. One pit is open to the public and descending the 30ft shaft on a vertical ladder is quite an experience, not to mention a challenge! Once down, you can view several horizontal galleries that radiate out from the main shaft. It is incredible to think that these mines were once dug by our ancient ancestors using antlers as picks and animal shoulder blades as shovels.

The Crossroads

The crossing place of two paths has long been associated with magic, haunting and the realm of other-worldly folk. A crossroads located outside a village was commonly used as a burial site for suicides, criminals and outsiders; and was often the place where the gibbet was situated.

This association with violent death and as a resting place of the lawless and heathen gave rise to the belief that it was a place where souls could not rest, and a place frequented by the devil and witches. Being a place of liminality, a threshold, a place that is betwixt and between, made it somewhere that otherworldly beings and fey folk would meet. It was also a place where pacts were made – often of the supernatural or lawless kind. Most crossroads were considered to have a guardian and offerings were left to appease them.

The powerful energies created by two different routes converging made them a place of energy and magic; and particularly good places for dispelling spells and charms. More recently crossroads are associated with making decisions and taking fate into your own hands, as the choice of where to travel next is yours.

The Highwayman of Nesscliffe, Shropshire

'Wild' Humphrey Kynaston, born in 1474, was the son of the High Sheriff of Shropshire who owned Myddle Castle. On inheriting the castle, he quickly went bankrupt due to wild living and sought refuge in the caves at Nesscliffe and became a highwayman. He is reputed to have drunk at the 'Three Pigeons Inn' which survives to this day and where you can still sit in his seat. He was declared an outlaw after being found guilty of the murder of John Hughes at Stretton.

In the true fashion of highwaymen, he stole from the rich and gave to the poor, and had a trusty steed named Beelzebub. Some believed him to have an allegiance with the devil because of amazing feats he was reputed to have accomplished: jumping over a huge gap in Montford Bridge crossing the River Severn, which had deliberately been sabotaged in an effort to try and catch him; jumping from the top of Nesscliffe and landing at Ellesmere, some nine miles away; and leaping over a section of the River Severn which is 40 ft wide and is now called Kynaston's Leap.

In 1518 he was pardoned by the King and lived out his days more quietly until his death in 1534. Nesscliffe is now a country park where you can visit the cave where Humphrey and Beelzebub lived and walk through the woods up to an ancient hill fort.

The Aberystwyth Mermaid

Early one morning in July 1826, a farmer from the parish of Llanfarian, Aberystwyth saw a beautiful young woman bathing naked in the sea close to his home. He turned away quickly to preserve her modesty, but after a few moments realised that she must be standing in deep water. He decided to take a better look, so he dropped to the ground and slowly crept forward, where he watched her for a good half an hour.

Eventually he rose and ran back to his cottage to raise his family and servants who followed him back to the place, some being only half-dressed because of the hour, and together they spied upon the strange maiden. When his wife arrived puffing and blowing with the effort of hurrying, she startled the creature, who up-ended, flicked her tail and swam away.

They followed the mermaid for a mile and half along the coastal path. Twelve people bore witness to this strange event and reported that she was 'exactly the same as a young woman of about 18 years of age, both in shape and stature, her hair was short and dark in colour; her neck and arms were like those of any ordinary woman, her breast blameless and her skin whiter than that of any person they had ever seen before'. The farmer, who had seen her for the longest, declared he had seen 'few women as handsome in appearance as this mermaid'.

Dinas Emrys, Gwynedd

Dinas Emrys, a hill near to Beddgelert in Wales, is named after Myrddin Emrys, who was known in England as Merlin. It is the site of one of the earliest stories relating to Merlin and involves the 5th century warlord of the Britons, Vortigern, who was trying to build a fortress on the summit. Each day progress was made, but every night the walls crumbled to the ground.

Vortigern consulted the Druids who advised that a boy, born of a human mother but sired by an incubus (evil spirit), must be found and sacrificed. Merlin, whose father was of supernatural origin, was chosen. The young boy told Vertigern that his men must dig down to a cave where two dragons fought every night in a chest where they were imprisoned; as their fighting was making the hill shake and the fortress crumble. All was as Merlin had described and when Vortigern opened the chest he found a red dragon and a white dragon. The creatures had one final battle, resulting in the red dragon winning and becoming the symbol of Wales, and the white one flying away to England.

Vortigern completed the fortress and rewarded Merlin by giving it, and the hill, to him. This is a wonderful place to visit in a truly magical area and has a path leading to the top where the foundations of an iron-age hill fort can be seen.

The Sin Eater

The tradition of 'sin eating' is so old that no one knows when it first began. The act of sin eating was taken on by a villager, who then became an outcast and lived beyond the village boundaries. Eating food and drinking over the corpse of someone who had died, and who had not made a confession, was meant to transfer the sins from the dead body into the sin eater, who kept them as a stain upon their soul. These people were usually rewarded with money from the deceased's family; and even though they were outcast, they were still maintained by the village because of the importance of their role.

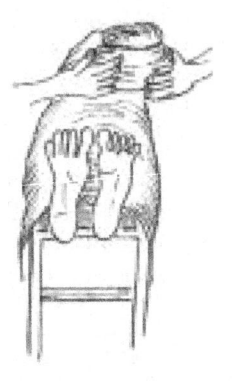

At the onset of a more vigorous Christian religion there is evidence to suggest that this practice continued and the church turned a blind eye. The last sin eater was Richard Munslow who, unusually, was buried in the churchyard at Rattlinghope, Shropshire in 1906. He was not an outcast, but a local farmer who was married and had children. These words are attributed to him, 'by eating bread and drinking ale, and by making a short speech at the graveside, the sin-eater takes upon himself the sins of the deceased'. The speech he would recite at the grave was written as: 'I give easement and rest now to thee, dear man. Come not down the lanes or in our meadows. And for thy peace I pawn my own soul. Amen'.

Roseberry Topping, North Yorkshire

Roseberry Topping is a wonderfully named hill with a very distinctive shape; a half cone with a jagged edge that can be seen for miles around. Unfortunately, it is also an area associated with a tragic tale of destiny.

King Oswald of Northumbria and his Queen were blessed with a baby boy, Prince Oswy. One night, the Queen fell into a fitful sleep and began to dream that her precious son would drown on his second birthday. When she awoke, her dream still seemed so vivid that she believed it must be an omen. She told her husband, who immediately sought counsel with his wise men. Each one told the King that the child must be removed to a place of safety, well away from any water. In due course, the Queen took the boy and climbed Roseberry Topping, the highest hill within their kingdom. Believing her son to be safe at last, the Queen fell into an exhausted sleep, yet unbeknown to anyone, a natural spring bubbled close to the summit.

Consumed with grief, the Queen died of heartbreak soon afterwards. Her husband decreed that the boy and his mother should be laid to rest together, at a place to be re-named 'Oswy-by-his-mother-lay' in remembrance of his family, now known as Osmotherley.

Will o' the Wisp

Strange, mysterious lights and flames often appear in wetland areas, fens, bogs and marshland areas across Britain. They are known by many names: Will o' the Wisps, Peg-a-Lantern, Hinky Punk, Will the Smith, Pinket, Jack-a-Lantern, Spunkies, Hobbedy's Lantern, and Jenny with the Lantern. The dancing lights are said to seek out lonely travellers and lure them away from the well-trodden, safe paths and lead them to certain death in the treacherous marshes.

Several regional explanations exist explaining their existence, but the most common seems to be that they are malevolent spirits of the dead who, for some reason, have become trapped between the worlds of heaven and hell and are doomed to wander the 'in between' for eternity, with just a single light for comfort. In some areas they are believed to appear in places where a tragedy is about to occur. Fen dwellers believed that if they saw one, they should lie face down on the ground until the light danced away. In reality, the dancing flames can be explained as a result of spontaneous combustion. Small pockets of naturally-occurring methane gas created by rotting vegetation ignite and then glow for a short while before fading away.

Edmund & the Wolf

According to the Anglo-Saxon Chronicles, Edmund landed at Hunstanton, Norfolk and claimed the throne of East Anglia in 854 AD. He was a popular King and well-loved by his people. His reign was terrorised by Viking invasions and eventually came to an end in 869 AD when he was slain by Ivar the Boneless during an attack at Diss. The Vikings tortured the King and tried to force him to deny his beliefs which he would not do. Finally, they killed him by shooting many arrows into his body which was then thrown onto a rubbish tip and his dismembered head thrown into the woods for the animals.

Later, a man wandering in the woods was attracted by calls of 'Hic, Hic, Hic' meaning 'here' and was surprised to see a huge she-Wolf. On looking closer he saw the head of his King untouched by the animals and realised that the wolf had been standing guard protecting the King's head. The wolf moved aside to let him retrieve the head so that it could receive a proper burial.

Coinage distributed much later in 986 AD depicted the King and a cult developed around his martyrdom. A shrine to Edmund became a place of pilgrimage for many including King Canute. You can visit the site where Edmund landed in Hunstanton which is marked by an oak carving of the sheWolf with her head raised to the moon.

Halliggye Fogou, Cornwall

The word 'fogou' originates from the Cornish 'ogo' meaning cave and suggests a natural structure, however the underground passages and spaces of Halliggye Fogou are most definitely manmade as they are roofed and lined with stone. This extensive Iron Age structure is situated just on the The Lizard and requires a torch to explore as it is completely dark, in fact this blackness combined with a low ceiling, uneven floor and chilled atmosphere make it quite an adventure to view. The chamber ends with a 'creep', an area of reduced height divided by a doorway of large slabs of stone.

The reason for building such structures is unknown; it is speculated that they acted as a store, refuge or ritual shrine. 'Finds' such as a vase containing ashes, a roughly-made cup and animal bones have all been found within Halliggye Fogou.

During the Second World War, the Fogou was used as an arsenal to store explosives and ammunition. Halliggye Fogou is one of the most elaborate and best-preserved of the fifteen structures of this type known to exist in Cornwall.

Burton Agnes Hall, North Yorkshire

This is a very old house, its origins can be traced back to 1173. During the time of Sir Henry Griffith, the hall was built and his daughter Katherine (Anne) Griffith was so taken with the new design that she could think and talk of nothing else - it was to be the most beautiful house ever built. One afternoon, Anne decided to visit some neighbours who lived closeby, but she was set upon and robbed. She was brought home but her life was in mortal peril. She drifted in and out of consciousness, sometimes raving, sometimes sane. She knew that time was short and begged that a part of her body be allowed to remain in the house forever. She was forceful and eventually persuaded her shocked sisters to agree to let her severed head be preserved within the fabric of the house.

A short time later Anne died but her family reneged on their deathbed promise, preferring instead to inter her remains within the churchyard. Aggrieved, Anne could not rest and her ghost appeared to the family. Scared out of their wits, they spoke to the vicar who eventually agreed that the grave be exhumed and her skull be brought to the house. Everything remained quiet until an attempt was made to remove her skull and bury it in the garden; the ghost of Anne returned with terrible clamour and upheaval. To this day, Anne's skull lies somewhere within the house, probably within the old walls but nobody knows for sure but her ghost is quiet and she is at peace.

Wayland Smithy, Wiltshire

This is one of the most impressive and atmospheric Neolithic burial chambers in Britain. Originally an oval mound covered a wooden and stone structure paved with Sarcen stones. Around 3500BC, the mound was enlarged to a trapezoid shape and was edged with Sarcen slabs. It had a façade of six larger stones, two of which are now missing at the southern end. A passage lined with stone was built within its southern face with two chambers forming a cross.

It was common for ancient monuments to be attributed to supernatural figures and this ancient grave somehow became associated with Wayland, the Saxon god of metalworking. It is well known that the art of smith was shrouded in mystery, legend and magic and it was said that if you leave your horse and a coin, it will be shod on the next morning of your return.

According to legend, Wayland sent his apprentice Flibbertigibbet on an errand to buy some nails. On his way back Flibbertigibbet was distracted by searching for bird's eggs, returning to Wayland hours later than expected. Angry, Wayland picked up one of the giant Sarcen stones and threw it at his apprentice pinning him by the heel. Unable to move Flibbertigibbet sat crying on the stone which is now known as 'sniveling corner'.

Zennor Mermaid, Cornwall

In the mediaeval church at Zennor is a carved chair. A mermaid is depicted on the sides of the chair, holding a mirror in one hand and a comb in the other.

According to legend, many years ago a richly dressed and beautiful lady occasionally attended the church at Zennor. Nobody knew who she was or where she came from. With such beauty, the lady had no shortage of want-to-be suitors in the village; one of them was Matthew Trewella, a handsome young man with the best singing voice in the village. After service one Sunday, the lady smiled at Matthew and he decided to follow her as she made her way towards the cliffs. The young man never returned to Zennor!

Years passed by until one Sunday morning a ship cast anchor off Pendower Cove. The ship's captain was on the deck when he heard a beautiful voice hailing him from the sea and he saw a beautiful mermaid. She asked him if he would raise his anchor as it was resting on the doorway of her house and she was anxious to get back to her husband, Matthew and he children.

A mermaid was carved into a chair and placed in the church, as a warning to other young men of the dangers or merry-maids and too commemorate these strange events.

Rollright Stones, Oxfordshire

This stone circle comprises seventy seven stones known as the King's Men. Outside the circle is the King's Stone and three other standing stones nearby are known as 'The Whispering Knights'. It is said that they are plotting against the King because of the incline towards each other.

According to legend, a King rode past the site and met a witch who said 'Seven long strides thou shalt take, and if Long Compton thou shalt see, King of England thou shall be'. He then took his seven strides, but as he was about to take his last, a mound rose up in front of him blocking his view. The witch chanted 'Rise up stick, and stand still stone, for the King of England thou shalt be none. Thou and thy men hoar stones shall be and I myself the Elder Tree'. Immediately the King and his men were petrified forming the stones we see today.

Another custom associated with the stones is that women can increase their fertility if the touch the stones with their bare breasts at midnight. Standing in the middle of the King's Men is meant to increase the power of prayer. Some believe that King Arthur lies beneath and the stones and the 'Rollrights' ate the Knights of the Round Table who lie sleeping, silently waiting for the signal that will rouse them and save England from her peril.

Kilpeck Church, Herefordshire

The church of St. Mary and St. David, located at ilpeck, Herefordshire dates back to at least 1140. It is believed that the church was built on the site of an earlier Saxon church which also has evidence of Celtic foundation. Some believe that it pre-dates this and could even be a megalithic site.

This particular church is renowned for its intricate carvings which depict pagan and Christian imagery nestling alongside each other in perfect harmony. The church escaped the attention of the Puritans and remains a very good example of the style and type of imagery used on the interior and exterior of parish churches. Together with Green Men, there are Basilisks, Dragons, Angels, Serpents and a Hare and Hound and a Sheela-na-gig. The south door tympanum depicts the Tree of Life.

Apart from demonstrating the skills of local craftsmen, the meaning and reasoning of the varied images is not known, but is believed to demonstrate an attempt to bring familiar deities of pagan and early Christian beliefs together to encourage as many of the local people to attend religious services as possible.

ABOUT THE AUTHOR

Anne Marie Lagram is an artist and folklorist. She has been interested in both since a child. She spends much of her time helping other artists and keeping alive the old ways and promoting the folklore of the British Isles, especially the folklore of Shropshire.

Printed in Great Britain
by Amazon